Speaking for Ourselves

Women and Distance Education in India

Speaking for Ourselves

Women and Distance Education in India

edited by

Asha S. Kanwar

Neela Jagannathan

MANOHAR

1995

ISBN 81-7304-112-1

First Published 1995

Published by
Ajay Kumar Jain
Manohar Publishers & Distributors
2/6, Ansari Road, Daryaganj
New Delhi - 110002

Lasertypeset by
A J Software Publishing Co. Pvt. Ltd.
305, Durga Chambers,
1333, D.B. Gupta Road,
Karol Bagh, New Delhi - 110005

Printed at
Efficient Offset Printers
215, Shahzada Indl. Complex
Delhi - 110035

CONTENTS

Acknowledgements

We express our sincere gratitude to Prof. G. Ram Reddy, Chairman, ICSSR, Ex-Chairman, the University Grants Commission and former Vice-Chancellor, the Indira Gandhi National Open University (IGNOU) for writing the foreword of this book. We are indebted to Dr. P. Rangaramanujam, Reader in Distance Education at IGNOU for reading and commenting on the 'Introduction' and the 'Select Bibliography'. We deeply appreciate the technical assistance received from Mr. Ajay Gupta, Deputy Director, Project Control and Mr. H.S. Harinarayana, Assistant Librarian, IGNOU. Our thanks are due to Mr. Gajendra Prasad Singh, Ms. Jasbir Kaur, Ms. Mandip Kaur Ahluwalia, Ms. Pushpa and Ms. Sushma Kohli for wordprocessing the chapters. Our appreciation is also due to the writers for responding so promptly and positively to our request for contributing papers. And last but not least, our sincere thanks to Mr. Ramesh Jain of Manohar for bringing out the book in record time.

Foreword

In recent years issues concerning the place of women and the problems faced by them in various walks of life have been highlighted by activists and scholars and as a result of their efforts the gender issue has come to the front burner of the social debate. While in the developed countries, one notices sensitivity to the gender issue, such awareness is yet to be created in most developing countries. There are several explanations for this, but the fact remains that the reality has to be faced by policy-makers and academics and suitable strategies have to be evolved, first to sensitize people about the problems of women and then to bring about changes in the existing situation. It is not enough to change policies and enact laws. The whole approach—the attitudes, language and culture—has to change, for the gender bias is deeply rooted in the psyche of the people. Take the case of the language of the UNESCO Charter which is otherwise a very progressive document. It says that "...since wars begin in the minds of men, it is in the minds of men that the defences of peace must be constructed...." The statement has one of the two implications:

a) only men and not women think of wars: or

b) the authors of the document have consciously or unconsciously used sexist language.

I leave it to the readers to draw their own conclusions. My own feeling is that the language has not been used carefully. I don't blame the authors because there was no sensitivity to sexist language when the UNESCO charter was drafted—and that has been the position for centuries.

The world—particularly the first world—has come a long way from that position. Still there are areas which are far behind the others and one such area is distance education. This book edited by

Asha S. Kanwar and Neela Jagannathan expresses the concerns of women in distance education in India. The contributors to the volume are all experienced persons in distance education and they focus on important aspects of the topic: Women and distance education in India. They cover a wide range of themes—from the position of women in educational policies and programmes to distance education for women: an international perspective and the Indian experience.

Asha Kanwar in her very stimulating 'Introduction' invites attention to such issues as the state of women's studies, gender and distance education in India, the need for empowerment, "self awareness and confidence". Her focus is on problem areas in distance education such as enrolment, retention, programmes, pedagogy and research. The authors raise issues which deserve the serious attention of policy-makers in distance education. For instance, why do women tend to have more dropout rates than men? Is it because they "lack self-esteem" and are "more inhibited and less articulate"? Similarly the types of programmes and their contents have a bearing on the response of women to distance education.

Distance education offers exciting possibilities for the empowerment of women. It transcends some of the obstacles which are inherent in the conventional system. However, as various articles in the book suggest, distance education has to remove some of its own obstacles and become user-friendly. This message is loud and clear in this book. I congratulate the editors and the contributors for choosing the theme of women in distance education and raising the problems confronting women. A beginning has been made by them and I am sure many others would be stimulated by their work. Finally, it is a book (except the Foreword) by women but it is not for women alone—men have a great deal to learn from it to purify their souls.

New Delhi
February 12, 1995

G. Ram Reddy
Chairman,
ICSSR

INTRODUCTION

Asha S. Kanwar

Research in distance education is still at an embryonic stage. Being a late yet important entrant on the educational scene, distance education is still engaged in a struggle to establish its credentials vis-a-vis conventional educational institutions. As such most initiatives in this area concentrate on introducing the virtues of the system in terms of its cost-effectiveness, use of high technology, flexibility, and more recently, quality. Such research is often carried out by men, who constitute the majority at each level of the hierarchy as administrators, teachers, counsellors, support staff and students. If we look at the four recent issues of the *Indian Journal of Open Learning (IJOL)*, we find that the majority of the contributors are men and the areas of interest can broadly be subsumed under the aforementioned areas. Of the 31 articles published to date, only four are authored by women, five more being co-authored with men (*IJOL*, 1992, 93). 'Gender Equality in Distance Education: An Analysis of Course Materials of IGNOU' featured in this book is the only article that focuses on the gender question. What this highlights, among other things, is the fact that research on and for women in distance education in India is negligible.

What then is the situation in the West? Karlene Faith's *Towards New Horizons: International Perspectives in Distance Education* (1988) was an important intervention in drawing attention to issues concerning women in distance education globally. In addition, the Women's International Network, a sister organisation of the International Council of Distance Education has attempted to bring together women from different parts of the world on a common platform from time to time. Its latest initiative in collaboration with the University of Umea, Sweden was to hold an International

Conference on 'Feminist Pedagogy and Women - Friendly Perspectives in Distance Education' in June 1993. Of the 25 women, representing different nationalities, there was a clear divide on the concerns of First World and Third World women. While research by women from the First World was grounded in sophisticated theory, papers by Third World Women were primarily descriptive and voiced basic concerns such as the struggle for instituting Women's Studies, convincing policy makers of the need for implementing women-related initiatives and the continuing struggle for equality.

Seeing that the concerns of the men on the one hand and Western women on the other lie in different directions, it became clear that we must take the initiative to edit a book that would bring together women's views on various aspects of gender and distance education in India starting from the visibility or otherwise of women in educational policies in post-independence India, to questions of empowerment and equality not only in open universities but also in other institutions such as correspondence courses institutes and SNDT university. With the exception of five articles, which have been published elsewhere, all the other chapters have been specially solicited for this volume. This has been done to cover general topics related to educational policies as in the first chapter by C. Shesharatnam, their implementation, women's empowerment and gender equality dealt with in the next three chapters; research into identifying need-based programmes for women; specific programmes and courses; gender bias in course content, language and graphics; pedagogy; support services in distance education and their implications for women. Having dealt with some of these areas we look at the role of distance education in the first women's university in the country, SNDT which Uma Vandse represents in her piece as well as in correspondence courses dealt with by Jamuna Thiagarajan. And finally we have Janet Jenkins assessing Indian distance education within the international context and looking towards the future. The contributors, are located in different institutions: B.R. Ambedkar Open University, Central Institute of English and Foreign Languages, University of Madras,

Institute for Social and Economic Change, Shrimati Nathibai Damodar Thackersay Women's University, Commonwealth of Learning and Indira Gandhi National Open University. With this wide representation we hope to present an overview of the current concerns of women vis-a-vis distance education in India.

As the contributors in this book are all women, does it mean that only women can articulate the experiences and concerns of women? While we do not wish to fall into the essentialist trap, it would be pertinent to ask here that if men can also express the concerns of women why is it that so few men have hitherto articulated women's concerns? Just as the book is not essentialist it is not separatist either. *Speaking for Ourselves* indicates that rather than being spoken for, we need to take the initiative ourselves. For as Audre Lorde has put it:

and when we speak we are afraid
our words will not be heard
nor welcomed
but when we are silent
we are still afraid
So it is better to speak.... (hooks, 129).

Conditioned into being seen rather than heard, coming to voice is an act of transgression, an act of resistance, an act of transformation, in short, a step towards self awareness and confidence. As Belenky et al. have pointed out women in general ground their epistemology in 'metaphors suggesting speaking and listening which is different from the visual metaphors such as illumination, insight used by scientists and philosophers' (Belenky et al. p.3). Women do have a predilection for dialogue and interaction from an early stage in their development. It helps them to reach out and connect. This book is a polyphonic coming together of different voices representing different ages and backgrounds. Therefore the "ourselves" signified in the title is not a monolithic entity for even though most women are located in academia yet the perspectives, voices, points of view are heterogeneous.

While it is clear that Third World women have concerns different from their sisters in the First World, and that even within the Third World women have different perspectives based on their race, class, caste, certain generalizations can be made about the subject category 'woman' within patriarchal societies. As far as apprehending reality is concerned, Belenky et al. have shown in their pathbreaking book *Women's Ways of Knowing* that women do indeed have ways of knowing different from men. Basing their study on intensive interviews and case studies, they have described "five different perspectives from which women view reality and draw conclusions about truth, knowledge and authority" (Belenky et al., p.3). These are:

> *silence*, a position in which women experience themselves as mindless and voiceless and subject to the whims of external authority; *received knowledge*, a perspective from which women conceive of themselves as capable of receiving, even reproducing, knowledge from the all-knowing external authorities but not capable of creating knowledge on their own; *subjective knowledge*, a perspective from which truth and knowledge are concerned of as personal, private and subjectively known or intuited; *procedural knowledge*, as a position in which women are invested in learning and applying objective procedures for obtaining and communicating knowledge; and *constructed knowledge*, a position in which women view all knowledge as contextual, experience themselves as creators of knowledge, and value both subjective and objective strategies for knowing.
>
> (Belenky et al., p.15)

While these stages can be found in the development of men as well and are by no means universal, as Belenky et al. admit, they are extremely useful in establishing that women's development processes are different. However Lorraine Code believes that presenting these five stages in women's intellectual emancipation "reinforces the essentialist tone" (Code, p. 260). She herself engages critically with mainstream epistemology, primarily the work of white male philosophers, in order to show how women have been pushed into positions of intellectual inferiority by the premises that underlie western institutions. She concludes:

> Knowledge is crucial to every aspect of human lives; its possession is empowering, its deprivation enervating and disabling. Women have to be in positions where they can know, if they are effectively to challenge the oppressions that have shaped their lives. Epistemologies have to be constructed that can produce these emancipatory effects (Code, xii).

And epistemologies that would reflect the concerns of women would be able to change the bases of our institutions which have hitherto excluded and silenced them. For as Adrienne Rich so aptly sums up: 'What we have at present is a man-centered university, a breeding ground not of humanism, but of masculine privilege'.

However, we speak here also of "open" universities which are avowedly based on principles of "equality" and "openness" with often the express mandate of reaching out to the marginalized and the dispossessed, which include both men and women. While the basic principles are progressive enough, the keyword here is effective implementation. This concern for implementing policy documents is voiced by Shesharatnam, Kanwar, Neela and Kamala in the first four chapters. Active intervention would be required in several areas if the distance education experience is to be made more gender-inclusive. These areas are enrolment, retention, programmes, pedagogy and research.

Enrolment

How can we enrol more women into distance education institutions? As we know, in India women learners do prefer off-campus study. Statistics show that 34.3% women go in for distance education as opposed to the 29.6% who opt for campus education (UGC Report). Christine von Prummer tells us that "It is usual for 'open universities' in industrialized Western countries that women constitute upwards of 40% of the student population, or even the majority of students as is the case at the Canadian Athabasca University." (Prummer, p 8). Distance education then seems to be preferred not just in India but more or less globally by women.

While there are several reasons for preferring home study, lack of confidence and independence is certainly an important factor. But paradoxically, studying at a distance also presupposes an independence and a degree of confidence that are prerequisites of autonomous study. However, successful completion of a programme would be empowering and hence it becomes imperative to introduce incentives so that more women can take advantage of these institutions. Publicity using all available media—print and electronic—as well as personal contact at the district and block levels can generate greater awareness regarding different programmes. Fee waivers, subsidies and scholarships would make distance education additionally attractive to women, who often have to surrender their educational aspirations in the face of economic constraints since they are, more often than not, financially dependent. Eligibility criteria need to be reviewed in terms of age, educational qualifications and experience, for women are often late-starters. In addition, the concept of the "neighbourhood" study centre must be examined so that women do not have to travel far in order to receive counselling. Recruiting women counsellors would help attract more women to counselling sessions. In addition to phased counselling sessions scheduled over a period of time, summer or winter school sessions of connected time must also be provided as an alternative to students, who may prefer this option. Inclusion of these options would certainly make distance education more attractive to women.

Retention

Having attracted women to the distance system, how do we keep them there? Research has shown that women rather than men have higher dropout rates. Women lack self-esteem, are more inhibited and less articulate. But they are also more motivated and determined to succeed. As such they need constant reinforcement and encouragement to sustain their initial motivation. Women can be easily de-motivated and as such sympathetic evaluation and assessment methods are required. In the chapter "Reaching Out: The Role of Counselling", Pushpa Ramakrishna concludes that counselling is beneficial to women as it can help them to build a 'positive self-image'. Stressing the importance of counselling, Manjulika Srivastava in 'Support Services and Women' tells us that these resources need to be further strengthened by opening more study centres, recruiting trained counsellors and providing a flexible time schedule. It is interesting to note that the recommendations suggested here are similar to those of Christine von Prummer of the Fern Universitat, who calls for "more flexible opening times and times for tutorials and counselling; help with the care of children...either through the provision of facilities or through financial support; providing students with the means to set up support networks, study groups and other forms of contact" (Prummer, p.21). Childcare has hitherto been the responsibility of the extended joint family in India but with the increase in the number of nuclear families, this aspect needs equal consideration in India. Support networks too would have different implications in this country as lack of telephone facilities, which are a convenient means of contact, are still not universally available. That contact is especially relevant to the woman learner has been demonstrated by von Prummer, Kirkup and Spronk who say that "women more than men, prefer to study in groups, and have contact with other students and staff" (p.57). Support services are only one aspect of the total responsibility towards making distance education more women-friendly. Assignments and evaluation systems also need to be made more attractive and relevant to the women learner.

Programmes

Which programmes would attract and retain women students? Should there be specific courses for women or should they be encouraged into more male-dominated options? And if so how? It is a commonplace to suggest that more women prefer "soft options" rather than professional courses in management, science and technology. Women's position in society has conventionally pushed them into socially accepted roles as homemaker, teacher, nurse whereas men are depicted as managers, decision makers, scientists, technologists. Rather than subvert such stereotypes, the hidden curriculum in our institutions often reinforces the same. For example, it is generally believed that most women do not prefer maths or science. Instead of using this to demonstrate that women have an inferior understanding, the question that needs to be posed is not what is wrong with girls that they cannot study science but what is wrong with science teaching that alienates girls? Two Norwegian male physicists, researching the problem, found "that if physics had been taught in another way with more emphasis on everyday experiences and on social and political questions girls would not have dropped out" (Brock-Utne p.32). Real-life experiences of women need to be built into the courses so as to invest the contents with the necessary relevance. Programmes in Women's Studies need to be instituted not as peripheral or token additions but as central priority areas. For by omitting the dimension of knowledge pertaining to one-half of the world's population, we would be faltering in our search for the whole truth. For the word "university" derived from "universitas" means the whole, the total (Gloria Bowles, p. 39). As such programmes reflecting the concerns of men and women would provide a whole, total curriculum. Past experience indicates that women-related programmes have the propensity for floundering on the questions of "cost-effectiveness" and "academic relevance". Being "interdisciplinary" in nature, they often become the site of control by contending departments and self-serving careerism. So initiatives often get undermined, subverted or coopted as patriarchal ideology prevails.

Regarding the courses offered by a distance education institution, would we continue to offer conventional academic courses at the tertiary level or would we need to extend the definition of a university to include functional literacy programmes as well? Shobhita Jain's proposal for a programme on Forest Management for Tribal Women indicates a possible solution to such dilemmas. The trend that seems to be emerging shifts the focus from catering solely to an elite enclave to diversifying into hitherto prohibited areas so as to reflect the needs of women in a developing country. Distance education should cater to basic literacy, functional literacy, legal education, health education etc. Research identifying these needs must be carried out as Mukta Prahlad suggests in her contribution. Neela Jagannathan and Uma Kanjilal focus on how Library and Information Science courses can be made more women friendly.

Not only must courses be framed to cater to the specific needs of women, care needs to be taken to ensure that the linguistic and graphic content of the course materials must be non-sexist and unbiased. Towards this end the UKOU has prepared a booklet. *Equal Opportunities Guidelines for Language and Image* (1993) which is circulated to "3,000 full-time and 6,500 part-time staff" (Kirkup and Taylor, 1993, p.180). Research has shown that women respond more favourably to texts that have gender-inclusive language (Ontario Women's Directorate, 1993). Kirkup and Taylor have pointed out that especially in distance education "the appropriate use of language is perhaps more important since the student learns through text and broadcast media" (p.178). The use of non-sexist language and non-biased graphics are dealt with in the chapter by M. Ushadevi.

Pedagogy

While non-biased language and ideologically sound images alongwith need-based course content can help women to relate to distance education course materials on a more realistic basis, the dimension of how these courses are taught, will help to either empower or alienate. For as Richard Shaull points out in his introduction to Paulo Freire's book:

> Education either functions as an instrument which is used to facilitate the integration of the younger generation into the logic

> of the present system and bring about conformity to it, or it becomes 'the practice of freedom', by means of which men and women deal critically and creatively with reality and discover how to participate in the transformation of the world (Freire, p. 13-14).

This blue-print for a "pedagogy of the oppressed" has special implications for a feminist pedagogy that would lead to the 'practice of freedom' by instilling in the learners an oppositional point of view (hooks, pp. 49-50). This point of view would challenge any form of domination and oppression - whether it is based on race, class, caste or gender. A feminist pedagogy would then aim to develop a critical consciousness that would penetrate the ideology that retails gender disparities as 'real' and 'natural'. In general, many women students suffer from a crisis of confidence and pedagogic strategies must enable the learner to view herself not from the sexist angle that she is generally seen from but as a human being complete, whole and undiminished. This would mean challenging not just our colleagues and students but first and foremost our own assumptions. For we often internalise the dominant ideology, not only echoing it but also producing the conditions of its future generation. Therefore what we need to do is to become aware of the 'piece of the oppressor that lies within us and uproot it' (Audre Lorde). More important than any other concern should be to displace 'entrenched thought structures' (Code p. 263).

Breaking out of socially imposed conditioning would lead to the empowerment of the learner. 'Empowerment', the new buzz-word has a politically correct aura. But what does it mean? At a seminar on empowerment, Nelly Stromquist defines it as:

> the ability to analyze the surrounding environment in political and social terms; it also means the ability to organize and mobilize for social change. In consequence, an empowerment process must involve not only individual awareness but collective awareness and collective action (Stromquist, p.5).

Empowerment then is a process that involves a range of activities. It is on the basis of knowledge that a learner will become aware of her social and political environment, which she will be able to analyze critically. This will motivate and encourage her to change the structures of exploitation not only within herself but also around her. Empowerment then does not have just an individual connotation but a collective one and implies going beyond narrow individual concerns towards becoming responsible members of society. This definition of empowerment is compatible with Paulo Freire's vision of education as 'the practice of freedom'.

How can this be done in concrete terms within the context of distance education? Some of the ways are: deconstructing the issues of power and domination by dispelling the teacher-learner hierarchy. Research in this area has shown that women respond more 'in settings where learning is a communal activity shared equally by students and teachers' (Brock Utne, p. 49). The authority of the printed word must be questioned and the learning process must become more participatory. Rebecca Coulter points out that 'course material should be designed in such a way as to overcome the criticism that the authority of the printed word and the patriarchal structuring of instructional design make distance education particularly difficult for women' (Coulter, p.15).

In short, by inviting the learner to engage critically with the study materials and relating these to their own lives will help in the process of empowerment. Renu Bhardwaj argues that the principles of experiential learning can help develop a feminist pedagogy. Different learners have different methods of learning. How can we cater to the heterogeneous and varied needs of a large corpus of learners? Field research in this area would provide useful inputs into pedagogic strategy.

It seems that feminist pedagogy then really is progressive pedagogy for what it strives to challenge is not just sexist domination but all forms of oppression. It is as valid in the classroom as it is in distance teaching institutions. In the latter, in fact, in becomes much more important as its effects are far-reaching and the learners, legion. The transformative potential thus becomes unlimited. In order to operationalise these principles, a great deal of awareness, coordination, commitment and bonding is required not only among the women but among all the men and women involved in the total process. Policy makers would have to prioritize these issues, pursue the implementation in terms of preparing guidelines and building them into faculty development programmes. It might be pointed out that most policy makers and the majority of those who decide the nature of courses, their content, course writing, counselling are men, as M. D. Ushadevi has shown. Inducting more women at all levels may, to some extent, help generate a more balanced reflection of male-female interests.

Research

Research into how pedagogy and curriculum development can become gender-inclusive and reflect the interests of women as well needs to be taken up seriously. And this research would have to be undertaken by men and women. From tentative beginnings of an "introductory" nature we would need to move away from description to rigorous analysis supported by critical theory. Women have often shied away from theory on the grounds that it is esoteric, jargonistic, intimidating. While there is theory that can answer to such a description, it is clear that this cannot be generalised bell hooks calls for the production of visionary feminist theory. This she explains, "emerges only from a context in which there is either an integration of critical thinking and concrete experience or a recognition of the way in which critical ideas, abstractly formulated, will impact on everyday life experience" (p. 39). Theory does provide a necessary analytic framework and can be empowering rather than emasculating if rooted in experience. Distance education is a new area and viewing it from the gender perspective makes it even more so. There are few models to follow and fewer authorities to invoke. This opens up infinite possibilities for women who are often rendered mute by long-standing traditions and the "canons" of the 'great masters'.

Finally, one wonders about the consequences of producing

such a book. Will it empower its contributors? Will it encourage other women? Will it help men become less sexist? Or distance education more gender-inclusive? Will it draw attention to the *causes* of sexism? Will it make a difference to institutional policy? For my own part, this is only a first step and if it can draw attention to the issues raised, it will have adequately served its purpose. Meanwhile, the voices that come together here are only a faint echo of 'that roar which lies on the other side of silence' (George Eliot, p.226).

REFERENCES

Belenky, Mary Field, Clinchy, Blythe McVicker, Goldberger, Nancy Rule, Tarule, Jill Mattuck (1986). *Women's Ways of Knowing : The Development of Self, Voice and Mind.* Basic Books, Inc.

Code, Lorraine (1991). *What Can She Know? Feminist Theory and the Construction of Knowledge.* Ithaca : Cornell University Press.

Coulter, Rebecca (1989). 'Women in Distance Education : Towards a Feminist Perspective' in Robert Sweet (ed) *Post-Secondary Distance Education in Canada : Policies, practices and priorities.* Alberta : Athabasca University and Canadian Society for Studies in Education, 11-22.

Eliot, George (1981). *Middlemarch.* Harmondsworth : Penguin.

Freire, Paulo (1972). *Pedagogy of the Oppressed.* Harmondsworth: Penguin.

Hooks, Bell (1989). *Talking Back : Thinking Feminist, Thinking black.* Boston : South End Press.

Indian Journal of Open Learning (1992,1993), Vol. 1 Nos. 1 & 2. January and July 1992 and Vol. 2, Nos. 1 & 2 January & July 1993.

Kirkup, Gill and Taylor Lee (1993). 'Does an Equal Opportunities Policy Support Women's Initiatives? : Case Studies from the Open University of the UK' in *Feminist Pedagogy and Women-Friendly Perspectives in Distance Education.* Sweden :

Women's Studies Center of Umea, Series of Reports No. 4, 166-184.

Kramarae, Chris and Reichler, Paula A. (1990). 'Power Relationship in the Classroom' in Gabriel, Susan and Isaiah Smithson (eds). *Gender in the Classroom : Power and Pedagogy.* Urbana: University of Illinois Press, 41-59.

Lie and Sjoberg (1984). *"Soft" girls in "Hard" Science.* Oslo : University Forlaget in Birgit Brock Utne, 'Feminist Didaktik the why, what and how to Teach women'. *Feminist Pedagogy....,* 29-56.

Mani, Gomathi (1989). *Women in Distance Education - Issues and prospects* Madras : Unicef.

Rich, Adrienne, (1979). *On Lies, Secrets and Silence : Selected Prose 1966-1978.* NY: WW Norton, 125-55.

Stromquist, Nelly (1993). The Practical and Theoretical Bases for Empowerment. Paper presented at the International Seminar on Women's Education and Empowerment, organized by the UNESCO Institute for Education, Hamburg, January, 1993, 19.

UGC Report 1973-74 (1976). New Delhi : UGC Printer.

Von Prummer, Christine (1993). 'Women-Friendly Perspectives in Distance Education' in *Feminist Pedagogy and Women-Friendly Perspectives in Distance Education,* 4-28.

Von Prummer, Kirkup and Spronk (1988). 'Women in Distance Education in D. Sewart and J.S. Daniel (eds.). *Developing Distance Education.* Oslo: ICDE, 57-62.

WOMEN IN INDIAN EDUCATIONAL POLICIES AND PROGRAMMES

C. SESHARATNAM

> "The realization of the country's aspirations involves changes in the knowledge, skills, interests and values of the people as a whole. This is basic to every programme of social and economic betterment of which India stands in need.... If this 'change on a grand scale' is to be achieved without violent revolution......there is one instrument, and one instrument only, that can be used: Education."
>
> **-The Education Commission, 1964**

Education reduces inequalities in society and leads to equalisation of status between individuals. Based on this, the Universal Declaration of Human Rights included education as the basic right of every human being. Equality of educational opportunity regardless of race, sex or any distinction, economic or social is an universal ideal. The Indian Constitution recognised the critical role of education in social transformation and promised equality of educational opportunities for men and women. But the history of Indian education during the past four decades does not reflect the fulfilment of the Constitutional aspirations and directions and goals of developmental plans. The following data drawn from Government documents illustrate the low educational status of women:

- constitutional target of free and compulsory education for all children up to the age of fourteen years remains unattained.
- literacy among women is lower than that among men. The rate of illiteracy among women is 60% as compared to 36%

among men (Table -1). Illiterate women predominate in villages and particularly among the underprivileged sections of society. The illiteracy rate is as high as 91% among SC and ST women. According to the 1991 census, out of 452 districts in the country in 115 districts the female literacy rate is lower than 20%. Barmer district in Rajasthan has just 6% female literacy rate, the lowest in the country.

- variance in education levels among female literates is high (Table - 2)—about 62% of the girls in the age-group of 6-14 years remain outside school.
- proportion of rural girls outside the ambit of formal education is as high as 70%. Even in urban areas, about one-third of the girls are outside the school system.
- the gap between the enrolment of boys and girls exists at all levels of education.
- the enrolment rate is poor among the girls of Scheduled Castes, Scheduled Tribes and other educationally backward communities. Females from poor families are born poor and continue to be poor and the formal system of education bypasses them.
- retention rates for girls in primary classes are low (Table - 3).
- the representation of women in higher education is as low as 31% . Of all the women enrolled in higher education, 55% are in Arts courses and only 20% in Science courses. More women join lower professional courses as compared to men. Only 6% of students enrolled for Engineering courses are women.
- the proportion of women teachers at primary, middle, higher secondary, college and university levels in 1980-81 was as low as 33%, 42%, 39% and 23% respectively (Table - 4).
- the percentage of women in the total enrolment in higher education in 1987-88 was 31% (Table - 5).
- women are poorly represented at higher levels of the decision making process in the education system.

- poorer sections of women get an unfair deal in the education system whose ethos is oriented to the needs and aspirations of the socially advantaged upper and middle classes.
- schools reflect and strengthen the traditional prejudices through their curricula, classification of subjects on the basis of sex and the unwritten code of conduct enforced on their pupils.
- research studies on women's education are negligible.
- women's studies in educational institutes and research centres are either discouraged or neglected.

The reasons for the low educational status of girls and women are many. The National Plan of Action for Women formulated by the Government of India (1976) identified the following major reasons for the slow development of women's education:

- general indifference to the education of girls.
- social resistance arising out of fears and misconceptions that education might alienate girls from traditions and social values and lead to maladjustments, conflicts and non-conformism.
- early marriage and social inhibitions against girls pursuing education after marriage.
- prevalence of child labour among girls belonging to weaker sections and the hard domestic chores which some of the unmarried girls are required to perform.
- prevailing notions that the sole occupation of women is to bear children, look after her husband and children, and thus be restricted to domestic work.
- discrimination against women's labour in both organised and unorganised sectors in matters of recruitment, training and promotion.
- many girls and their parents find that the school curriculum does not conform adequately to their needs and interests.
- unsuitable and inflexible school timings and inadequate

facilities for girls in schools, particularly in co-educational schools.

The above and other socio-economic factors responsible for the low educational status of women have been studied, investigated and reviewed in the post-Independence period by various Committees and Commissions and many suggestions have been made by them for the enhancement of the educational status of women. The notable among such bodies are:

1) University Education Commission, 1948.
2) Secondary Education Commission, 1952.
3) National Committee on Women's Education, 1958.
4) Committee on Differentiation of Curricula for Boys and Girls, 1964.
5) Education Commission, 1964.
6) Committee on the Status of Women in India, 1974.
7) Committee to Review the National Policy on Education, 1990.
8) Committee to Review the National Policy on Education, 1991.

The suggestions and recommendations of these bodies formed the basis for the formulation of educational policies and plans. Among the policies and programmes of the Government of India on education which incorporated policies on women's education, the important ones are:

1) National Policy on Education, 1968.
2) Blueprint of Action and National Plan of Action for Women, 1976.
3) Draft National Policy on Education, 1979.
4) Women in India: Country paper, 1985.
5) National Policy on Education, 1986.
6) Programme of Action, 1986.
7) National Perspective Plan for Women, 1988.

8) Programme of Action, 1992.
9) Five Years Plans.

Let us see briefly the significant policy perspectives and programme contours perceived and practised in the country for the development of women's education.

National Policy on Education, 1968

In July 1968, the Government of India issued the National Policy on Education based on the recommendations of the Education Commission, 1964 and the Report of the Committee of Members of Parliament on the Education Commission. This was the first national policy on education evolved and announced by the Government of India after independence on education. This Policy raised many hopes among educational administrators, educationists and the general public. The Policy enumerated seventeen broad principles to guide the development of education in the years ahead: 1) free and compulsory education, 2) status, emoluments and education of teachers, 3) development of languages, 4) equalisation of educational opportunity, 5) identification of talent, 6) work experience and national service, 7) science education and research, 8) education for agriculture and industry, 9) production of books, 10) examination, 11) secondary education, 12) university education, 13) part-time education and correspondence courses, 14) spread of library and adult education, 15) games and sports, 16) education of minorities, and 17) educational structure. Under the fourth principle 'equalisation of educational opportunity' it stated that: "the education of girls should receive emphasis, not only on grounds of social justice, but also because it accelerates social transformation." Unfortunately the Policy did not mention more than this on the education of girls and women. The policy failed to highlight the new areas of change needed for enhancing the visibility of women in educational development. In general, the Policy was far from satisfactory.

Draft National Policy on Education, 1979

The end of the 70's saw the next major policy of the Government on education. The first ever non-Congress Government at the Centre, with a view to reshaping the 1968 Policy, drafted a new national policy in 1979. The Policy could not get a final shape as the non-Congress coalition government did not complete its full term in power. Though the Draft Policy desired "recasting of the contents of education at all levels so as to make the education process functional in relation to the felt needs and potentialities of the people", on girls' and women's education, the Draft had hardly said anything radical. In the chapter on universal elementary education the Draft included girls under the category of disadvantaged sections which also included scheduled castes and tribes, landless labourers, backward classes and urban slum poor and suggested special attention to the education of these sections. Referring to the need for the expansion of adult education, the Draft Policy stated: "Since the programme is not only meant for removing illiteracy alone but its aim is also to create awareness about other problems, it would be desirable that such programmes as family planning, health and nutrition, child and mother care should be built into this programme. For this it would be desirable that the newly appointed instructors for the programme should be women as far as possible." Surprisingly this policy too failed to look at women's education from a broad perspective of human resource development. Thus, the policy perspectives of the national government in the first three decades of post-independence were narrow.

National Policy on Education (NPE) and Programme of Action (POA), 1986

The National Policy on Education (NPE) 1986, was a landmark in the approach to women's education. It attempted for the first time to address itself to the basic issues of women's equality. In the section titled 'Education for Women's Equality' the Policy stated:

"Education will be used as an agent of basic change in the status of woman. In order to neutralise the accumulated distortions of the past, there will be a well-conceived edge in favour of women. The National Education System will play a positive, interventionist role in the empowerment of women. It will foster the development of new values through redesigned curricula, textbooks, training and orientation of teachers, decision-makers and administrators and the active involvement of educational institutions."

The National Policy soon after its adaption by the Parliament in 1986 was followed by the Programme of Action (POA) which was meant to provide an indication on the nature of actions needed to implement the directions of the Policy. The POA spelled out the meaning of Women's empowerment in the following words:

"Women become empowered through collective reflection and decision making. The parameters of empowerment are:

- building a positive self-image and self-confidence;
- developing the ability to think critically;
- building up group cohesion and fostering decision-making and action;
- ensuring equal participation in the process of bringing about social change;
- encouraging group action in order to bring about change in the society;
- providing the wherewithal for economic independence."

The following measures were indicated for the achievement of the above:

a) Every educational institution should by 1995, take up active programmes of women's development built around a study and awareness of the women's predicament and for promotion of communication and organisation among women.

b) All teachers and Non-Formal Education/Adult Education (NFE/AE) instructors should be trained as agents of women's empowerment. Special training programmes will be developed by NCERT, NIEPA, Directorate of Adult Education (DAE), SCERTs, State Resource Centres (SRCs) and UGC to incorporate in all training programmes of teachers and NFE/AE instructors elements which would motivate them to work for women's empowerment. Voluntary agencies and activist groups for women's development will be involved in these training programmes.

c) Women teachers and women instructors in Adult Non-Formal Education Programmes should receive special orientation to enable them to play an activist role towards women's equality.

d) Special programmes should be developed by research institutions, voluntary institutions and professional groups of artists to promote general awareness and self-image among women through a variety of programmes like discussions, street plays, wall papers, puppet shows etc.

e) An environment should be created in which practically all sections of the society will commit themselves and work for achieving the objectives enunciated in the National Policy on Education. Keeping in view the important role played by media in this sphere, clear policy guidelines should be developed by radio and TV in 1986-87 and measures taken to persuade films and other media on these lines.

f) Preference in recruitment of teachers upto school level should be for women. This will create a greater confidence in the rural areas and motivate the parents to send girls to school.

g) The common core curriculum is a powerful instrument for the empowerment of women through the incorporation of values commensurate with the new status of women. The Women's Cell in the NCERT will be revived and given the responsibility for preparing the component of the core curriculum relating to women's equality. The Cell should also accelerate its work of eliminating sexist bias and sex stereotypes from school textbooks. The Women's Cell of NCERT should take the active help of all persons on playing its assigned role.

h) Sensitisation of teachers, trainers, planners and administrators to women's issues will be taken up as a major programme by NIEPA and appropriate State Level agencies, through initial training, in-service training and refresher courses. NIEPA should also have a strong cell for the planning and execution of these programmes.

The POA aimed at the promotion of a four dimensional (teaching, research, training and extension) Women's Studies programmes as indicated below:

1) Teaching:
- incorporation of issues relating to women's status and role in the foundation course proposed to be introduced by University Grants Commission for all undergraduate students;
- incorporation of the women's dimension into courses in different disciplines;
- elimination of sexist bias and sex stereotypes from textbooks.

2) Research:
- encouraging research on identified areas and subjects which are crucial in advancing knowledge and to expand the information base;
- critical appraisal of existing research tools and techniques which have been responsible for the disadvantages suffered by them and where necessary information of research methodology.

3) Training:
- dissemination of information and interaction through semi-

nars / workshops on the need for Women's Studies and its role in University education;

- orientation of teachers and researchers to handle women-related topics and to incorporate women's dimension into general topics;
- workshops for restructuring the curriculum.

4) Extension:

Programmes such as adult education, awareness building, legal literacy, informational and training support for socio-economic programmes of women's development, media, etc. which would directly benefit the community and women.

The POA hoped that :

> the interventions and programmes referred to above would be planned, coordinated, monitored and evaluated continuously both at the national and state levels. Each of the organisations responsible for the programme will have to be strengthened. The Women's Cell in the NCERT will be revived and stengthened. NIEPA and Directorate of Adult Education will have strong cells to plan and administer women's training programmes. The Women's Cell in the UGC will be strengthened in order to monitor the implementation of various programmes at higher education level. At the State level, Women's Cell should be set up in all the States with adequate supporting staff to be headed by an officer of at least Joint Director's status.

Some efforts were initiated immediately after the adoption of the Policy and the issue of POA to bring in changes at primary and secondary levels of education by bringing into existence schemes like Navodaya Schools. However, despite these resolutions, the policies still need to be implemented in order to prove effective.

National Perspective Plan for Women (1980-2000), 1988

The Perspective Plan for Women prepared by the core group set up by the Department of Women and Child Development, Ministry of Human Resource Development, Government of India was an effort for a long term policy for Indian Women guided by the Constitutional principles and directives relevant to the development process. The Plan did not see women as the weaker section of society or as passive beneficiaries of the development process. It viewed them as a source of unique strength for realising national goals.

With a view to giving a new thrust and responsiveness to multi-dimensional development programmes the Plan recommended specific interventions for women as transitory measures to ensure that they catch up with the mainstream by 2000 AD. The thrust of the Plan was fivefold: (a) strengthening and vigorous implementation of existing legislation, (b) reorientation of programmes to serve the aim of achieving parity not only between men and women but also between different sections of the women themselves, (c) recasting policies and programmes to serve the special needs of women, (d) special interventions to enhance accessibility to benefits due for women and, (e) empowering women to absorb the benefits meant for them.

Considering the multiple roles of women in society, the Plan aimed at the following measures for the development of education by 2000 AD:

- awareness needs to be generated among the masses regarding the necessity of educating girls so as to prepare them to effectively contribute to the socio-economic development of the country, to strengthen their role in society and to realize their own capacities. The media and various forms of communication have to be geared to this end.
- involvement of local leaders, voluntary agencies and women's groups is necessary. An incentive scheme should be introduced to motivate panchayats to ensure 100 per cent enrolment of girls in their respective villages.
- for improving enrolment and minimising dropout rates and

wastage in case of girl students, it would be helpful if learning is made more attractive by providing adequate teaching materials in schools.

- the number of teachers should be increased so that the interaction between the teacher and the taught, which is so essential for good education increases. In single teacher schools the teacher must be a woman. In the case of two teacher schools, at least one teacher must be a woman.
- school curricula should be imaginatively developed to stimulate creativity. Regional language should normally be the medium of instruction.
- school timings should be flexible to suit local conditions and the needs of the working girl and must be available within walking distance of the child. A substantial increase is required in the number of schools for girls.
- in addition to incentives like free textbooks, free supply of uniforms, awards of attendance, scholarships and midday meals, facilities such as proper school building, safe drinking water, and toilets, etc. need to be provided to encourage school enrolment and retention of girls.
- local talent must be developed for recruiting women teachers at the primary and elementary levels especially in rural and tribal areas. In this endeavour national agencies like CAPART and CSWB voluntary agencies, mahila mandals and local self government agencies can make a significant contribution. They can also play a useful watchdog function to ensure that educational and other programmes are run efficiently and effectively.
- there should be a reservation of 50 per cent posts for women teachers in elementary schools. Women teachers working in the rural areas should be provided suitable accommodation.
- multi-entry system for girls who cannot attend schools continuously should be adopted.
- wherever necessary, schools exclusively for girls may be set up. The recommended distance of three kilometres for

locating a middle school is a handicap for many girls. To ensure participation of girls in middle schools, it is necessary to provide hostel facilities.

- many girls in the 11-14 years age group would first have to be brought into the primary stage through non-formal education.
- special efforts are necessary for bringing tribal children, particularly girls into the school system. Tribal dialects, extreme poverty, problems of commuting, rigidity of formal education and its irrelevance to the tribal culture and the tribals' distrust of the ways of the mainstream society, must be borne in mind in formulating strategies.
- non-formal education is an alternative to the formal system with the potential of becoming the major programme of education for girls who cannot attend school during normal school hours due to various reasons.
- diversified courses leading to occupational preparation should be of parallel duration to the general secondary courses. In addition, there should be a variety of short and long term, full-time, part-time and apprentice courses:
- general and vocational training courses should be combined so that prospects of a career immediately on completion of schooling may attract girls from weaker sections. While designing the vocational courses, available occupational opportunities as well as the need to overcome market stereotypes should be kept in view.
- correspondence courses and self-study programmes can be especially useful for girls desirous of continuing education but are unable to do so because of circumstances.
- the open school system should be expanded extending the facility to all the girls in rural and backward areas.
- secondary schools for girls must be helped to build good science programmes over the Eighth Five Year Plan. Special scholarships for girls opting for science courses need to be instituted at the secondary and higher education levels.
- there is a need to open more colleges and polytechnics for

girls, especially in rural areas.

- incentives like scholarships, freeships etc., should be provided to enable girls from rural areas to pursue higher education. For girls belonging to weaker sections, in addition to freeships and scholarships, bursaries should also be provided to meet their requirements for food and lodging.
- reservation of seats for girls in professional courses may be considered to remove the existing bias in access to certain professional streams.
- the women's wings of the universities could undertake large scale extension programmes in order to activate girls and women in the surrounding areas to take advantage of educational and occupational facilities of various types, particularly those leading to meaningful employment, essential for reducing women's marginalisation.
- in order to increase the representation of rural girls in higher education courses, 30 per cent seats, may be reserved for girls to begin with.
- all agencies involved with the preparation of curricula, prescription of textbooks and organisation of educational processes will have to evince awareness towards women's issues. University/College departments of Women's Studies, appropriate voluntary agencies, women's groups, etc. should be involved in giving a new perspective to the various issues of content and processes of education. Women's Universities and Women's Centres in colleges need to take an active role in women's development and in influencing the attitudes of future generations.
- facilities for part-time self study and correspondence courses should be provided on a large scale to enable girls who are not in a position to join higher educational institutions on a regular basis to continue their studies.
- entrepreneurship development programmes should be organized separately for the education of women in the age group of 18-30 years, with a minimum of matriculation level of education. The objective of such training should be

to (i) make them aware of the various opportunities for self-employment; (ii) motivate them to take up self-employment; (iii) impart needed skills and training; (iv) promote motivation for achievement among them; and (v) create access to resources such as capital credit etc.

- adult education will have to be composed of three interrelated strands aimed at: (i) continuous flow of new information especially to rural and tribal reas, particularly to inculcate positive attitudes towards women, (ii) continuous training of the people in the use of modern tools and methods of production and, (iii) acquisition of permanent reading and computation skills.
- the growing availability of communication media should be directed to portray positive images of women in non-conventional roles. Involvement of mass media in motivating women to attend literacy classes is most essential.
- rapid strides in the development of technologies and tools for the reduction in women's drudgery and easy access to work places, water and fuel supply, childcare, health services and population control can contribute significantly to the success of learning programmes for women. Women's literacy programmes would succeed better if they centre around women's concerns.
- all women workers in industries or elsewhere should be made literate by the employers by allotting time from working hours for their education. Place of teaching, teachers and teaching material should be arranged by them. Necessary legislation to this effect may be enacted.
- the existing Integrated Rural Development Programme, National Rural Employment Programme, Developmment of Women and Children in Rural Areas, Training of Youth in Self-Employment Programmes, Integrated Child Development Programmes etc. should have a component of literacy for their women beneficiaries. Training should be provided to the functionaries of various development departments by the Directorate of Education in the States.

- State Resource Centres should produce suitable learning material for women on a priority basis. Literature for neo-literates should be suitably devised by experts, keeping in view the needs of different groups of learners.
- Decentralisation is the key to the successful application of the strategies outlined above. In this decentralised approach, the village cluster or the block level is seen as most appropriate for the delivery of programmes. It is, therefore, necessary that the block is allocated a flexible budget so as to make funds available to village clusters/villages for innovative educational activities and for equalisation of education opportunity.
- an overall coordination of health, welfare and educational inputs would be most desirable. This would entail (a) convergent policies in these sectors; (b) coordination of delivery mechanisms, and (c) pooling of allocations. The Perspective Plan was a comprehensive blueprint for enhancing the educational visibility of women. However, the change in the Government at the Centre and the consequent political events during 1989-91 pushed the Perspective Plan into the background.

Five Year Plans

The First Five Year Plan (1951-56) envisaged welfare measures for the women. The Second Five Year Plan (1956-61) continued the welfare approach. The Third Five Year Plan (1961-66) pinpointed female education as a major welfare strategy and the Fourth Five Year Plan renewed this emphasis. The basic policy was to promote women's welfare within the family as the base of operation. The Fifth Five Year Plan (1974-79) recommended a programme of functional literacy to equip women with skills and knowledge to perform the functions of a housewife. The plan coincided with the International Women's Decade and the submission of the Report of the Committee on the Status of Women in India (CSWI). A major outcome of the CSWI Report was the National Plan of Action

(1976) that identified education, among other initiatives, for formulating and implementing action programmes for women and called for planned interventions to improve women's condition.

The Sixth Five Year Plan (1980-85), for the first time in India's planning history, had a chapter on women and development. The Sixth Plan emphasised three strategies for women's development (a) economic independence; (b) educational advance; and (c) access to health care and family planning. This shift in terminology from welfare to development and the extension of women's areas of concern from the social services sector of education, health and welfare to the critical areas of economic development—agriculture, rural development, land rights, forest policy and access to training and investment resources for their fuller participation in independent economic activities—represented a major change. The Seventh Plan (1985-90), reflected the concern for equity and empowerment articulated by the International Decade for Women. For the first time, the emphasis was qualitative focusing on inculcating confidence among women; generating awareness about their rights and privileges; and training them for economic activity and employment. The Eighth Plan (1992-97) continued the Seventh Plan perspective which aimed at integrating women into mainstream national development.

Distance Education

To overcome the rigidities, compulsions and limitations of the formal system of education and to widen the access to educational opportunities, new efforts to develop non-formal education began in recent times. Women, who mostly remained outside the formal system for a variety of reasons, are expected to be beneficiaries of the non-formal education system. Distance education is a home-based and learner-centred form of education which is free from the constraints of time and place.

Distance education in its modern sense is of recent origin in India. The first course through correspondence for the Bachelor's Degree began at Delhi University in 1962. Most of the Institutes of

Correspondence Studies and/or Directorates of Distance Education are located in conventional universities. The University Grants Commission intended the correspondence courses to cater to the educational needs of (a) students who had to discontinue their formal education owing to pecuniary and other circumstances, (b) students in geographically remote areas, (c) students who had to discontinue education because of lack of aptitude and motivation but who may later on become motivated, (d) students who cannot find a place or do not wish to join a regular college or university department, although they have the necessary qualifications to pursue higher education, and (e) individuals who look upon education as a life-long activity and may either like to refresh their knowledge in an existing discipline or to acquire knowledge in a new area.

The Education Commission (Kothari Commission) which had a comprehensive look at India's education system recommended a more extensive use of correspondence education for a wide range of purposes. The 1970s saw the introduction of correspondence education in many universities. During the 1960s, only undergraduate courses were started whereas the 1970s saw the introduction of postgraduate and diploma/certificate courses as well. In 1987-88, there were about 33 universities offering correspondence courses in the country. Meanwhile a few universities like Mysore, SNDT, Women's University, Madurai Kamaraj, Andhra, Madras and Annamalai adopted open admission policies by relaxing formal qualifications for entry to undergraduate courses. This provided opportunities for many women to re-enter the higher education sector.

The first Open University in the country was established by the Government of Andhra Pradesh at Hyderabad in 1982 to provide access to higher education to adults to upgrade their skills, improve their quality of life, equalize educational opportunities and provide life-long education. The encouraging response to this University resulted in the establishment of other open universities in the country. The Indira Gandhi National Open University was set up in 1985 with the responsibility (a) to provide opportunities for higher education to larger segments of the population, particularly those for whom access to the formal system is difficult or impossible, (b) to develop the open university and distance education systems in the country and to coordinate and determine standards in such systems. In the last four years open universities have also been established by the State Governments of Rajasthan, Bihar and Maharashtra.

The National Policy on Education (1986) emphasized the importance of distance education and open university systems for augmenting opportunities for higher education and as instruments for democratizing education.

One of the broad objectives of distance education is to offer on a large scale educational opportunities to women who may either like to take up careers or like to further their education. That this objective is not being fulfilled is clear from available data. The data for 1989-90 (Table - 6) reveals that of the total enrolment in distance higher education institutes in India, females accounted for 41 per cent only. There are wide regional imbalances in the enrolment of women. The proportion of females in the Central and Western Region was 57 per cent, in the Eastern Region it was only 27.3 per cent. In the Southern and the Northern Regions, the proportion of females was 40 per cent and 41 per cent respectively. The sexwise break up of students reveals that distance education programmes have not equally benefited women and hence further expansion of the system is needed to attract more women. The states which have lagged behind in promoting women's education through distance education programmes are Uttar Pradesh, Rajasthan, Kerala, Bihar and Orissa. The regional imbalance in the development of distance education needs to be eliminated.

The Open Universities are to take the lead in providing more and better educational opportunities for women. Their present performance leaves much to be desired. Take for example, the case of Andhra Pradesh Open University. On the other hand, distance education institutions in Britain are playing a significant role in promoting women's education (Tables 7, 8 and 9). The Open Universities should design and develop innovative courses so that more women can be attracted to the system.

Impact of Policies, Plans and Programmes

A review of educational policies, plans and programmes formulated and implemented from time to time by the Central and State governments does not indicate the educational development of women in the desired direction. This is evidenced by the analysis of the educational profile of women.

- The female literacy rate, though improved from 8.9% in 1951 to 39.2% in 1991, is still low. In a state like Rajasthan it is less than 21%.
- The constitutional goal of universalisation of elementary education is not yet fulfilled.
- The enrolment of girls in schools is considerably low. According to the 1981 census, in the rural areas only 25.8% of girls in the age group of 5-9 years were going to schools, as compared to 55.6% in the urban areas (the overall figure was 32.2%). In the age group of 10-14 years, in the rural areas 44.3% were going to schools as compared to 65.5% in the urban areas (the overall figure was 50.4%). The inter-state differences are striking. The overall school enrolment ratio for girls was less than the all-India figure (37.5%) in several states.
- Attrition at the lower and primary stage is very high for girls as compared to boys. A study of the NCERT in 1971 on the problem of wastage and stagnation in primary and middle schools reported that the rate was 71.4% for girls and 62.3% for boys. CSWI found that of every 100 girls enrolled in Class 1 about 30 reached Class 5. Dropout and wastage continued to be high.
- The enrolment of girls improved steadily over the years but it is still 31.3% of the total enrolment. In the faculties of Engineering, Technology, Agriculture, Medicine, Veterinary Science, women's participation is limited.
- The National Adult Education Programme (NAEP) initiated in 1978 placed special emphasis on enrolling women

as students, instructors and decision makers. But resistance among men and the community, lack of time and energy among the poor women, inadequate number of women instructors and supervisors and absence of childcare facilities are hindering the progress in women's access to the programme.

- School curricula is still full of sexist biases. The value of equality through curricula is not yet recognised and promoted by educational institutions.
- Teachers are not oriented to promote gender equality through their teaching. Women's issues are not covered in research and teaching activities of higher education. Women's studies have not increased quantitatively and qualitatively.
- Distance education has not been very successful in bringing a large number of women into the education sector. Women's participation in higher levels of educational planning and decision making is marginal.

What is to be done?

The International Women's Decade in India witnessed unprecedented efforts from various organisations, areas and sectors to reassess the roles of women, to enlarge the information base, to search for alternative strategies for women's equality and development, and to develop policies and programmes addressed to women's specific problems and needs. The Committee on the Status of Women in India (CSWI) which undertook a "comprehensive examination of all the questions relating to the rights and status of women" in the context of "changing social and economic conditions in the country and new problems relating to the advancement of women" made the first major attempt to comprehend the trend of changes in women's status in the light of the Constitutional guarantees of justice, equality and fraternity, in its report titled "Towards Equality" submitted to the Government at the beginning of the Women's Decade.

In CSWI's view, "equality is an article of faith in our Constitution, and is necessary, not merely on the grounds of social justice, but as a basic condition for social, economic and political development of the nation. Disabilities and inequalities imposed on women have to be seen in the total context of the society where large sections of the population—male and female, adults and children—suffer under the oppression of an exploitative system. It is not possible to remove these inequalities for women only. Any policy or movement for emancipation and development of women has to form part of a total movement for removal of inequalities and oppressive social institutions...."

The CSWI made far-reaching recommendations for increasing the visibility of women in education. Thereafter the National Policy of Education (1986) and the National Perspective Plan for Women (1988) also recommended several measures for achieving women's educational equality. In practice all these policies, plans and programmes have not enhanced the educational status of women. Women's educational development is to be seen as a part of overall development and not in isolation. Yet, special efforts need to be made to improve the educational status of women.

As a step in this direction, it is worth recalling the important principles declared by the World Conference of the International Women's Year in 1975 on the equality of women and their contribution to development. These are:

1. Equality between women and men means equality in their dignity and worth as human beings as well as equality in their rights, opportunities and responsibilities.
2. All obstacles that stand in the way of enjoyment by women of equal status with men must by eliminated in order to ensure their full integration into national development and their participation in securing and in maintaining international peace.
3. Women and men have equal rights and responsibilities in the family and in society. Equality between women and men should be guaranteed in the family, which is the basic

unit of society and where human relations are nurtured. Men should participate more actively, creatively and responsibly in family life for its sound development in order to enable women to be more intensively involved in the activities of their communities and with a view to combining effectively home and work responsibilities of both partners.

4. Women, like men, require opportunities for developing their intellectual potential to the maximum. National policies and programmes should therefore provide them with full and equal access to education and training at all levels, while ensuring that such programmes and policies consciously orient them towards new occupations and new roles consistent with their need for self-fulfilment and the needs of national development.
5. The right of women to work, to receive equal pay for work of equal value, to be provided with equal condition and opportunities for advancement in work, and all other women's rights to full and satisfying economic activity are strongly reaffirmed.
6. All means of communication and information as well as all cultural media should regard as a high priority their responsibility, for helping to remove the attitudinal and cultural factors that still inhibit the development of women and for projecting in positive terms the value to society of the assumption by women of changing and expanding roles.
7. Equality of rights carries with it corresponding responsibilities; it is therefore a duty of women to make full use of opportunities available to them and to perform their duties to the family, the country and humanity.
8. Every couple and every individual has the right to decide freely and responsibly whether or not to have children as well as to determine their number and spacing, and to have information, education and the means to do so.
9. The issue of inequality, as it affects the vast majority of the women of the world, is closely linked with the problem of

underdevelement, which exists as a result not only of unsuitable internal structures but also of a profoundly unjust world economic system.

10. The full and complete development of any country requires the maximum participation of women as well as of men in all fields: the under-utilization of the potential of approximately half of the world's population is a serious obstacle to social and economic development.
11. The ultimate end of development is to achieve a better quality of life for all, which means not only the development of economic and other material resources but also the physical, moral, intellectual and cultural growth of the human being.

TABLE 1

LITERACY RATE: 1951 TO 1991

	MALES	FEMALES	COMBINED
POPULATION AGED FIVE YEARS AND ABOVE			
1951	27.16	8.86	18.33
1961	40.40	15.34	28.31
1971	45.95	21.97	34.45
1981	53.45	28.46	41.42
POPULATION AGED SEVEN YEARS AND ABOVE			
1981	56.37	29.75	43.56
1991	63.86	39.42	52.11

Notes : 1. Unlike earlier Censuses which had taken the literacy level for population aged five years and above, in 1991 Census these data relate to the population aged seven years and above.

2. The 1981 data exclude Assam while the 1991 data exclude Jammu and Kashmir.

TABLE 2

PERCENTAGE OF FEMALE LITERATES BY EDUCATION LEVEL

EDUCATION LEVEL	1961	1971	1981
PRIMARY	*29.6	38.2	32.7
MIDDLE	—	15.6	16.7
MATRIC/HIGHER SECONDARY	**4.6	7.9	12.4
NON-TECHNICAL DIPLOMA	—	0.2	0.1
TECH. DIP. & CERT. NOT EQUAL TO DEGREE	—	0.2	0.6
GRADUATE AND ABOVE	—	1.4	2.9
LITERATES WITHOUT EDUCATIONAL ATTAINMENT	65.8	36.5	34.8
ALL LITERATES	100.0	100.0	100.0

Source: Office of the Registrar General, India.
* Includes Middle.
** Includes matriculation and above.

Note: For 1981, figures exclude Assam.

TABLE 3

RETENTION RATES FOR GIRLS IN PRIMARY CLASSES

YEAR	CLASS	GIRLS
1970-71	II	60.7
	III	47.2
	IV	37.1
	V	29.1
1980-81	II	70.6
	III	61.6
	IV	51.6
	V	38.3
1985-86	II	77.2
	III	65.3
	IV	56.4
	V	51.0

Source: Ministry of Human Resources Development, Department of Education.

TABLE 4

PERCENTAGE OF FEMALE TEACHERS TO MALE TEACHERS AT DIFFERENT LEVELS OF EDUCATION

YEAR	PRIMARY SCHOOL	MIDDLE SCHOOL	HIGHER SECONDARY SCHOOL	COLLEGE AND UNIVERSITY
1950-51	18	18	18	8
1960-61	21	32	22	14
1970-71	26	37	26	18
1980-81	33	42	39	23
1988-89	39	50	42	NA

Source: Ministry of Human Resouce Development, Department of Education.

TABLE 5

TOTAL ENROLMENT AND ENROLMENT OF WOMEN IN HIGHER EDUCATION IN INDIA

YEAR	NUMBER OF UNIVERSITIES	NUMBER OF COLLEGES	TOTAL ENROLMENT	WOMEN ENROLMENT	PERCENTAGE OF WOMEN'S COLLEGES	NUMBER OF WOMEN'S COLLEGES	PERCENTAGE OF WOMEN'S COLLEGES
1970-80	119	4558	26,48,579	7,89,042	26.0	577	12.2
1980-81	123	4722	27,52,437	7,48,525	27.2	609	12.9
1981-82	131	4886	29,52.066	8,16,704	27.7	624	12.7
1982-83	133	5039	31,33,093	8,80,156	28.1	647	12.8
1983-84	139	5246	33,07,649	9,40,253	28.4	676	12.9
1984-85	140	5590	34,04,096	9,92,139	29.1	712	12.7
1985-86*	149	5816	35,70,897	10,58,612	29.6	741	12.7
1986-87*	155	6512	36,81,870	11,25,304	30.6	771	11.8
1987-88*	164	6597	38,14,417	11,95,073	31.3	802	12.1

* Estimated.

Source: Annual Report of UGC, 1987-88.

TABLE 6

SEXWISE BREAK UP OF DISTANCE HIGHER EDUCATION STUDENTS IN INDIA, 1989-90

REGIONS	MALE	FEMALE	TOTAL	PERCENTAGE	
				MALE	FEMALE
SOUTHERN REGION					
1. ANDHRA PRADESH	44,754	21,028	65,782	68.0	22.0
2. KARMATALA	15,682	6,850	22,532	69.6	30.4
3. KERALA	5,944	1,904	7,848	75.7	24.3
4. TAMILNADU	1,05,897	85,130	1,92,027	55.4	44.6
SUB TOTAL	1,72,277	1,14,912	2,87,189	60.0	40.0
NORTHERN REGION					
5. DELHI	22,675	18,481	41,166	55.1	44.9
6. HARYANA	7,427	11,533	18,960	39.2	60.8
7. HIMACHAL PRADESH	11,661	4,599	16,260	71.7	28.3
8. JAMMU & KASHMIR	1,201	684	1,885	63.7	36.3
9. PUNJAB	8,789	5,317	14,106	62.3	37.7
10. RAJASTHAN	5,935	1,985	7,920	74.9	25.1
11. UTTAR PRADESH	7,871	2,488	10,359	76.0	24.0
SUB TOTAL	65,559	45,097	1,10,656	59.2	40.8

TABLE 7

SEX WISE ENROLMENT OF ANDHRA PRADESH OPEN UNIVERSITY UNDERGRADUATE STUDENTS

ACADEMIC	MALE	FEMALE	TOTAL	PERCENTAGE	
				MALE	FEMALE
1983-84	5296	935	6231	85	15
1984-85	8387	2857	11244	75	25
1985-86	11291	4411	15702	72	28
1986-87	13762	5509	19271	71	29
1987-88	11295	5010	16305	69	31
1988-89	11499	5219	16718	69	31
1989-90	11366	5036	16402	69	31
1990-91	19966	7480	27446	73	27

TABLE 8

SEXWISE ENROLMENT OF STUDENTS IN DISTANCE EDUCATION INSTITUTES IN BRITAIN

NAME OF THE INSTITUTE	% MEN	%WOMEN
OPEN UNIVERSITY UNDERGRADUATES	54	46
OPEN UNIVERSITY ASSOCIATE STUDENTS	46	54
NATIONAL EXTENSION COLLEGE	37	63
NALGO CORRESPONDENCE COLLEGES/ INSTITUTES	65	35
PRIVATE CORRESPONDENCE COLLEGES	64	36

TABLE 9

PERCENTAGE OF WOMEN STUDENTS ON BRITISH OPEN UNIVERSITY UNDERGRADUATE COURSES (1988)

FACULTY	LEVEL	%WOMEN
ARTS	FOUNDATION	67
	2ND	66
	3RD/4TH	69
SOCIAL SCIENCE	FOUNDATION	63
	2ND	49
	3RD/4TH	54
EDUCATION	2ND	72
	3RD	66
MATHEMATICS	FOUNDATION	22
	2ND	23
	3RD/4TH	23
SCIENCE	FOUNDATION	35
	2ND	40
	3RD/4TH	41
TECHNOLOGY	FOUNDATION	26
	2ND	13
	3RD/4TH	13

DISTANCE EDUCATION FOR WOMEN'S EMPOWERMENT

ASHA S. KANWAR

Distance education has infinite possibilities, especially in the uplifting and empowerment of women. This chapter aims to address itself to the question of why, despite women's increased enrolment in educational institutions in post-independence India, there has been no concomitant uplift in their socio-economic position. Where then has our educational policy failed? Should there be a separate programme for women's education? And more specifically, how can distance teaching institutions work towards women's increased participation in the economic and developmental processes of the nation?

After 47 years of independence, only (39.9%, 1991 census) Indian women are literate. (Therefore, when we talk of higher education for women, we must remember that we are thinking only of this minority.) The Indian Constitution, progressive in spirit, stands committed to the equality of men and women. Yet gender disparities remain. The University Education Commission (1951) revealed its discriminatory bias when it perceived women's role in stereotypical terms: "... the greatest profession of women is, and probably will continue to be, that of a homemaker" (p 122). And if they wanted equal educational opportunities they would have to "forgo home and family." And which "good" Indian woman, the epitome of self-effacement and sacrifice, would want to do that? However, there is a slight concession in the report of the Education Commission (1966). This allows women the option to have access to both home and career, stating that women should be enabled to "carry out their dual role of home-making and following a suitable career" (p. 138). Here again there is no attempt to break out of the roles traditionally assigned to women. A more radical shift takes place in the recent "National Policy on Education" approved by the Indian government in June 1986, which focused on the problem of women's education in the following terms:

> Education will be used as an agent of basic change in the status of women. In order to neutralise the accumulated distortions in the past, there will be a well-conceived edge in favour of women. The National Education System will play a positive interventionist role in the empowerment of women. It will foster the development of new values through redesigned curricula, textbooks, the training and orientation of teachers, decision-makers and administrators, and the active involvement of educational institutions.... Women's studies will be promoted.... Major emphasis will be laid on women's participation in vocational, technical, and professional education at different levels. The policy of non-discrimination will be pursued vigorously to eliminate sex-stereotyping in vocational and professional courses and to promote women's participation in non-traditional occupations, as well as in existing and emergent technologies (p. 6).

But before we examine how this document can translate into a concrete action-plan to eliminate gender differentials, let us briefly survey the existing scenario. The participation of women in higher education in 1951-52 was only 12.3%, but by 1985-86 the percentage had gone up to 29.6% (UGC Report). It is clear that the number of educated women had increased, but has there been any substantial change in their status? Newspaper reports inform us almost daily about dowry deaths or more appropriately, dowry murders. Moreover, the report of the Committee on the Status of Women (1975) has underscored the facts that there has been increasing mortality among women and female children, that there has been greater unemployment of women after 1950 and that there has been a wider gap in the ratio of literacy and education between men and women. In spite of the increased educational opportunities available to women, their condition remains deplorable. The state has apparently spared no effort. There were only 22 universities in India in 1951. Less than four decades later we have over 160. It is clear that among other things access to education alone cannot ensure a basic change in status; it is ultimately the kind of emphasis and the kind of education provided that can effect attitudinal changes in society and the condition of women. In any case, women have limited access to these institutions. Within Indian culture, marriage and not education has been the final destiny of a woman. This is one reason why Indian women, trying to balance housework and academic pursuits, find distance education more suitable to their needs. According to a UGC Report (1976), there are 29.6% of women in college-based courses, whereas in correspondence courses there are 34.3%.

In order to provide a viable alternative channel of education, Indira Gandhi National Open University was established in 1985. One of the aims of the university is to provide access to higher education to the disadvantaged and marginalized sections of society. It further seeks to provide high quality education at minimal costs to the maximum number of people all over the country. It makes use of multi-media (print, audio and video) to reach out to its heterogeneous and diverse corpus of learners. Among other things, it is committed to minimizing the male/female divide. So far there are only 20.2% women on its rolls, which is less than the percentage of women enrolled in college-based or correspondence courses. A brief survey of the gender distribution of students in the various courses run by IGNOU is given in Table 1.

It is interesting to note that the Certificate on Food and Nutrition has the maximum enrolment of 62.9% women whereas the percentage drops to a paltry 5.5% in a professional course such as the Diploma in Management. The pattern of enrolment thus remains the same as in conventional institutions. According to one report, 59% of women opt for arts, 26.75% for commerce, 11% for education, while only 2.5% enrol in science courses (Mani, 1989, p 6).

Why is it that women choose conventional subject combinations rather than more professional courses? Women have been

TABLE 1
Gender Distribution of Students in IGNOU Courses
(1991-92)

Course	Total	(1991-92) Female		Male	
CFN*	5655	4292	(75.9%)	1363	(24.1%)
DIM*	7350	428	(5.8%)	6922	(94.2%)
DDE*	484	180	(37.2%)	304	(62.8%)
DCW*	468	206	(44.0%)	262	(56.00%)
BDP*	15104	413	(27.2%)	10991	(72.8%)

Source: Planning Division, IGNOU* (CFN, Certificate in Food and Nutrition; DIM, Diploma in Management; DDE, Diploma in Distance Education; DCW, Diploma in Creative Writing; BDP, Bachelor's Degree Programme).

known to choose options such as arts, education, nursing and if there are women who have opted for engineering, technology or computers, their number is minimal and they can only be seen as exceptions proving the rule. A career in teaching or nursing can be seen as an extension of women's traditional roles of nurturing: mother, sister or wife. The pattern of the sexual division of labour in patriarchal society thus infiltrates the sphere of education.

Therefore the choice of subjects in higher education is largely dictated by the socialization within the family, school and society. The sexism inherent in gender power relations is subtly inserted into textbooks and curricula. To illustrate this, let us look at examination questions, which according to Belsey (1983) are "the ultimate location of institutional power they identify the boundaries of the discipline, and define what is permissible to 'discuss'...". "Although concerned about the place of man in this universe and his predicament, Narayan is a comic writer. Do you agree?" (Panjab University, 1985, M.A. Part II); "Discuss The Rape of the Lock as a satire on the frivolities of women in contemporary society" (Panjab University, 1985, M.A. Part II). "Man", then, is a transcendental ahistorical category while "woman" is nonexistent as far as cosmic issues are concerned. "Woman" is defined in certain stereotypical and humiliating categories as frivolous, vain, the object of male contempt and occasional indulgence. By "interpellating" the female subject in such terms, patriarchal ideology is carrying out its function—not as "false consciousness" but as a belief system that structures and highlights the gender differentiation. Instead of performing a progressive role, education works as an "ideological operateur" (in Macherey's parlance) in the interests of maintaining the status quo.

Patriarchal ideology also ensures that even if a woman attains a high level of education, in terms of achievement, she is still liable to fall behind man. Wolpe (1978) suggests that "woman's ambition is tied to her role in marriage and to the goals directly related to marriage...." (p 297). This is clearly symptomatic of the

> internalisation of values which define adult male and female behaviour patterns...as an integral part of normal childhood development; and it is the internalisation of 'female' values which...affects woman's occupational attainment in adulthood (p. 302).

Among these values are submission, self-sacrifice and tolerance, while the specific personality trait congruent with achievement is "aggression", which is termed "masculine" and therefore in woman "deviant". These two polarities, the former a constant and the latter a variable, are traceable in contemporary popular culture. For example, popular TV serials like *Ramayan* set up the character of Sita as the paradigm of Indian womanhood. (As Romilla Thapar, the historian has pointed out, several versions of the *Ramayan* existed at different periods in history, but it is this particular version that gained prominence to the extent that it is generally taken as the only authoritative one. The role of ideology is clearly visible in suppressing the more independent Sita of the other versions.) On the other hand, recent cinema features the "angry young woman", aggressive and revengeful. While this image no doubt provides a valuable role model, in the last analysis it generally fails, as its thrust is diverted in the interests of conformity. Love is the controlling factor and is generally represented in Byronic terms: "Love to a man's life is a thing apart, 'Tis a woman's whole existence". Such notions result in a woman's return to submission and humility thereby vindicating patriarchal ideology. How then does one hope to "eliminate sex stereotyping" and promise "vocational and professional courses"? Can the resultant economic independence make a substantial change unless there is an overall change in societal attitudes dependent on a complex of factors? More pertinently, how can distance teaching institutions contribute to this enterprise?

As far as a specific programme towards educating women is concerned, IGNOU has introduced a Certificate in Food and Nutrition aimed primarily at women, though men are not excluded. Diploma courses in Food and Nutrition and Organizing Child Care have also been launched. These courses are subsumed under the category of Women's Education. That the objectives cover aims such as "acquiring skills for the maintenance of family" and "community's health" are indeed laudable in a developing third world nation where malnutrition is a major problem. But the problem with such programmes is the fact that individuals are "channelled into vocationally oriented courses such as technical skills or home economics on the basis of gender rather than individual aptitude" (Jayaweera, 1987, p. 464).

Such courses could simply come under the category "Home Science" with incentives to attract both men and women. It is for this reason that I would like to separate "Home Science" from "Women's Education". Women's Education must have a wider scope to include both basic and functional literacy. Programmes must be identified through extensive research in urban and rural sectors with the specific aim of training women for the job market or entrepreneurial projects. Teaching strategies would necessarily be dictated by the needs of the target group. For example, Allama Iqbal Open University, Pakistan, has used flip charts, audio cassettes and radio programmes with great success. Here the authority of the printed word is dispersed and non-literate women are able to participate. Courses such as these extend the definition of what a university is by encouraging the participation of women hitherto completely by-passed by our educational policies and programmes.

One of the reasons why women's access to education has not resulted in a concomitant change in status is partly because the thrust of our policies has not been to change the relations of production which subsume gender relations, but only to sympathize with the lot of women and to improve it with subsidies and other "discriminatory compensations". Such ad hoc solutions provide short-term remedies but fail to diagnose the basic causes. Instead of liberal reformist attitudes, a more radical approach is required so that the gender problem can be tackled not only vis-a-vis its internal dialectic but also within a wider context that would take into account the economic, ideological and political factors and their ramifications on educational policy.

An effective starting point in this project would be to introduce Women's Studies programmes. How do we define Women's Studies? This is an area of work whose two-fold function is seen as "a means by which women could produce knowledge about themselves, of their own history and condition" and project that knowledge by means of a "pedagogic practice" (Kuhn and Wolpe, 1978, p. 2). The Women's Studies programmes must be an autonomous entity so that it has "the potential to alter fundamentally the nature of all knowledge by shifting the focus from androcentricity to a frame of reference in which "women's different and differing ideas, experiences, needs and interests are valid in their own right..." (Bowles and Klein, 1983, p. 3).

Courses in Women's Studies must therefore be encouraged because they

(a) are interdisciplinary; this means for instance that a course on "Women in Indian Society" would require inputs from the fields of history, politics, sociology, literature and so forth;
(b) provide a fresh perspective;

(c) can validate academic study by relating its concerns to our contemporary cultural context and the concerns of women in society;
(d) can lead to consciousness-raising in gender-related issues; and
(e) prove more accessible to women students who can relate more easily to such courses.

As Kirkup (1988) puts it "the issue of access also relates to delivery systems, with content presented in new ways that will make it more accessible to women, through the way that it is written, with new examples and different perspectives or through the design of delivery systems, for example, scheduling tutorials to take into account family responsibilities (pp. 287-288).

Distance teaching institutions with a multi-media infrastructure at its command can play an interventionist role in the cultural life of the community by instituting a media-monitoring cell that scrutinizes and censors the sexism rampant in mass-media. The subject category "woman" has been artificially structured into stereotypes based on mediations by externalities such as market considerations, consumerism and control of third world economies, among others. Specific courses can be designed to expose and explode the so-called "feminine mystique" that pervades academic disciplines, mass-media and other cultural practices. Here the U.K. Open University (UKOU) course on "The Changing Experience of Women" would provide a useful guideline. But at this point it would be well to remember that the concerns of Indian women, living in a society based on caste, class and gender, must necessarily be different from their Western sisters. The mention of Women's Studies still generates resistance. It is precisely for this reason that the discipline demands serious consideration and institutional support.

Within our institutions, we could further undertake to vet the "he-man" language within our own study materials. A brief glance at the following statements will prove the necessity of such an enterprise: Baath (1984) suggesting guidelines for the tutor involved in distance education says that the tutor should be able to "individualise his tuition...." Mukta Prahlad, presenting a paper at the National Workshop on Women in Distance Education in India says that the distance learner has the responsibility "to keep himself working..." at self-instructional courses (Mani, 1989, p. 55). Clearly women are non-existent as both tutors and learners. To assume that "women" are subsumed under the rubric "men" is to highlight the invisibility of women and the general amnesia in relation to them within patriarchal society. To dismiss the vetting of sexist language as fetishistic hair-splitting is to forget that those who control language control reality. In order to disperse such linguistic androcentricity, it is essential to give this monitoring serious consideration.

Distance Education institutions can also explore ways and means whereby more women can be encouraged to join professional courses. One obvious way could be to provide financial incentives in terms of subsidies and scholarships. Another would be to include women in the content of the course on the lines of UKOU's Women into Management course. Such courses would not only be about women but also for women. It would also keep specific problems of women in mind while drawing up personal contact schedules. Moreover media can be used effectively to generate awareness among women regarding their rights and options by providing useful role models. In our society, at this point in time, such an exercise is imperative as most women still think within the parameters of their traditional social conditioning. Short optional courses on "Women and Law", "Feminist Historiography", "Women in Politics", "Literary Women", to name a few, could be introduced as a part of the overall project of effecting attitudinal change.

What can be done to encourage women's participation in distance teaching institutions both as teachers and as learners ? First of all, institutional and financial support is required for research projects concerning women in distance education. Gender is still a marginal factor in research in this area. Rather than following Western theoretical models, women in the developing world need to generate knowledge about themselves, in their own voices. Secondly, more programmes aimed at "reentry" women need to be developed with a focus on the 'need' rather than 'demand'. Women's experiences need to be written into the courses. In addition, a greater networking of women in distance education is required. Towards this end, a directory of Who's Who of women in distance education needs to be brought out.

Hiring and the upward mobility of women in distance education institutions is another area that needs attention. Like conventional institutions, the ubiquitous glass ceiling puts paid to many a promising bright female career. Women constitute 41% of the teaching staff at IGNOU: 2 Professors, 8 Readers, 55 Lecturers. It is clear that this is still not good enough. But the point is not simply the induction of women but the adoption of a feminist perspective that will unravel the ideological assumptions that underlie the production and distribution of knowledge. Distance teaching institutions can indeed effectively engage with the gender question both academically and socially as they have the requisite infrastructure to filter down to the very grassroots. Notions of what constitute a women's "nature" and a woman's "sphere" must be effectively challenged. Sexism is man-made and open to change. It is time to initiate the process.

REFERENCES

Baath, T.A. (1984). Research on completion and discontinuation in distance education. *Epistolodidaktika*, 1-2, pp 31-43.

Belsey, C. (1983, Spring). Literature, history, politics. *Literature and History,* 19(1), p. 17.

Bowles, G. and Klien, R.D. (1983). *Theories of women's studies.* London: Routledge.

Education Commision, India, (1966). *Report of the education commission 1964-66*. Delhi: Manager of Publications.

Jayaweera, S. (1987). Gender and access to education in Asia. *International Review of Education*, 33(4), pp. 455-467.

Kirkup, G. (1988). Sowing seeds: Initiatives for improving the representation of women. In K. Faith (Ed.), *Toward new horizons for women in distance education: International perspectives* (pp 287-312). London: Routledge.

Kuhn, A. and Wolpe, A. (1978). Feminism and materialism. In A. Kuhn and A. Wolpe (Eds.), *Feminism and materialism: Women and modes of Production*. (pp 1-10). London: Routledge and Kegan Paul.

Ministry of Human Resources Development (1986). *National policy on education*. New Delhi: Government of India, Department of Education.

Mani, G. (1989). Indian women in distance education. In G. Mani (Ed.), *Women in distance education - Issues and prospects* (pp 12- 19). Madras: Unicef.

Report of the National Committee, 1971-74 (1975). *Status of women in India*. New Delhi: Allied Publishers.

U.G.C. Report, 1973-74 (1976). New Delhi.

Report of the University Commission, 1949-51 (1951). Simla: Government of India.

Wolpe, A. (1978). Education and the sexual division of labour. In A. Kuhn and A. Wolpe (Eds.), *Feminism and materialism: Women and modes of production* (pp 290-328). London: Routledge and Kegan Paul.

GENDER EQUALITY AND EQUITABLE OPPORTUNITIES FOR WOMEN: IGNOU'S ROLE

NEELA JAGANNATHAN

Sex-bias is predominant worldwide in all the spheres of human activity including education. During the United Nations declaration of 1975 as the International Women's Year and 1976-85 as the Decade for Women, startling statistics came into light summarizing the position of women globally. It indicated that women constitute 30% of the official labour force, perform 60% to 89% of all agricultural work, produce at least 50% of all food, receive 10% of the World's income, possess less than 1% of the world's wealth (*The International Encyclopaedia of Education*- vol.1). Women and girls constitute 50% of the world's population and 75% of the world's undernourished (Gayfer, 1980).

These statistics are no doubt, distressing but there is a noteworthy improvement in the last two decades. This discrimination can be reduced only if the literacy percentage of women is raised. In most of the countries, attempts are being made to reduce the sex-bias and to improve the access of women to education.

According to a World Bank Report, in 2000 A.D., there will be 500 million illiterates in India constituting 54% of the World's population of illiterates. As per the Seventh Plan, the total number of adult illiterates is about 90 million of whom 58 million are women. These figures are very depressing. Again, the comparative statement of education among men and women as revealed in 1981 Census, depicts that there has been uneven development of education at various levels. The sexwise difference between enrolment of girls and boys till middle school is not much but from matriculation to university level, the percentage of women enrolment goes on decreasing drastically and the percentage of women dropouts goes on increasing due to varied socio-economic reasons. This was realised as early as 1962, when a Committee constituted by the Ministry of Education under the Chairmanship of Dr. D. S. Kothari, the then Chairman of the University Grants Commission to examine the feasibility of starting Correspondence Courses in India, rightly reported the absolute necessity of women's education in India:

> For the full development of our human resources, for the improvement of the homes and for moulding the character of the children during the most impressionable years of infancy, the education of the women is of greater importance than that of men.

Even the preamble to the United Nations on the elimination of discrimination against women stresses that:

> The full development of a country, the welfare of the World and the cause of peace require the maximum participation of women as well as men in all fields.

The new National Policy on Education (1986) is a landmark in the approach to women's education. It lays special emphasis on the removal of disparities and to equalise educational opportunity to all sections of the society. In the section entitled 'Education for Women's Equality', the policy states:

> Education will be used as an agent of basic change in the status of women. In order to neutralise the accumulated distortions of the past, there will be a well conceived edge in favour of women. The national educational system will play a positive, interventionist role in the empowerment of women. It will foster the development of new values through redesigned curricula, textbooks, the training and orientation of teachers, decision makers and administrators and the active involvement of educational institutions.

India being the vast, most populous, multilingual country with over 57% of its population being illiterate. Distance Education is the only viable alternative to promote higher education and bring it to the doorstep of those who are handicapped and underprivileged. Women, especially in rural areas, comprise the largest section of the under-privileged group in Indian society.

But in the last two decades there is a considerable rise in the sense of awareness for social equality among Indian women. They want

* to enhance social status by mixing with various people of diverse fields;
* to improve their economic condition and lifestyle;
* to have better promotional avenues at work; and
* to improve their educational qualifications which could not be done by joining a regular college.

In India, a large number of women are seeking admissions in the courses conducted by distance teaching institutions. Even the New Education Policy (1986) has stressed the importance of non-formal education using modern educational technology. In the 'Programme of Action' published in August 1986 it is stated that:

> The open university system augments opportunities for higher education, ensures access, is cost-effective and promotes a flexible and innovative system of education.

The Government of India is committed to restructuring the whole system of higher education. In fact, the Indira Gandhi National Open University (IGNOU) was established in September 1985 with the objectives of democratising education by extending equal opportunities to all sections of society and by reaching each and every corner of the country.

IGNOU has discarded the elitist approach to education found in the conventional universities. In turn, it has adopted an innovative and flexible system of education which has relaxed entry regulations, self-pacing in learning, no time-place barrier, freedom in choice of subjects etc. It has produced integrated multi-media packages by using modern communication technology. IGNOU's main aim is to impart, quality teaching through cost-effective course materials.

IGNOU has introduced diversified and flexible courses pertaining to liberal, professional and continuing education after conducting careful and systematic survey of the demands from various groups. The conventional as well as innovative academic programmes produced by the Schools lead to award of certificates, diplomas and degrees.

The academic programmes already launched by the University till 1992-93 are -

1. Certificate programmes in -
   - Food and Nutrition (CFN)
   - Guidance (CIG)
   - Rural Development (CRD)
   - Tourism Studies (CTS)

2. Diploma programmes in -
   - Computer Applications (DCA)
   - Computers in Office Management (DCO)
   - Construction Management (ADCM)
   - Creative Writing in English (DCE)
   - Creative Writing in Hindi (DCH)
   - Distance Education (DDE)
   - Higher Education (DHE)
   - Management (DIM & ADIM)
   - Nutrition & Health Education
   - Financial Management (DFM)
   - Human Resource Management (DHRM)
   - Marketing Management (DMM)
   - Operations Management (DOM)
   - Rural Development (DRD)
   - Water Resources Engineering (AWRE)

3. Bachelors Degree Programmes in -
   - Arts (B.A.)
   - Commerce (B.Com.)
   - Sciences (B.Sc.)
   - Library and Information Science (BLIS)
   - Nursing

4. Master's Degree Programmes in -
   - Business Administration (MBA)
   - Distance Education (MADE)
   - Library and Information Science (MLIS)

IGNOU's basic objective is to provide equal opportunities for higher education to all including industrial and agricultural workers, professional and other employees, people residing in urban, rural and tribal regions, belonging to upper class, lower class and weaker sections i.e. scheduled castes, scheduled tribes, backward classes, housewives etc.

It is too early to undertake any in-depth analysis of the students enrolment in various courses conducted by IGNOU. But from the available statistics of the students enrolled from different regions viz. rural and urban (See Table 1 : Regionwise Enrolment of Students : 1988-89 to 1992-93) and sections i.e. general, Scheduled Castes and Scheduled Tribes (See Table 2 : Sectionwise Enrolment of Students : 1986-87 to 1992-93), it is felt that IGNOU has not been very successful in fulfilling its objective of extending equal opportunity for higher education by attracting students either from remote, rural and tribal areas or from the weaker sections of the society.

TABLE 1
REGIONWISE ENROLMENT OF STUDENTS
(1988-89 TO 1992-93)

Year	Rural Number/Percentage		Urban Number/Percentage		Total
1988-89	5,723	13.52	36,601	86.48	42,324
1989-90	5,864	12.15	42,417	87.85	48,281
1990-91	9,702	18.52	42,674	81.48	52,376
1991-92	13,707	21.98	48,668	78.02	62,375
1992-93	15,792	20.87	59,874	79.13	75,666

TABLE 2
SECTIONWISE ENROLMENT OF STUDENTS
(1986-87 to 1992-93)

Year	General		Scheduled Caste		Scheduled Tribe		Total
	No.	%age	No.	%age	No.	%age	
1986-87	4,335	98.95	24	0.55	22	0.5	4,381
1987-88	15,321	91.13	1,213	7.22	277	1.65	16,811
1988-89	38,389	90.71	2,918	6.89	1,017	2.4	42,324
1989-90	43,834	90.79	3,170	6.57	1,277	2.64	48,281
1990-91	48,303	92.24	2,917	5.56	1,156	2.20	52,376
1991-92	58,609	93.97	2,504	4.01	1,262	2.02	62,375
1992-93	67,092	88.68	6,263	8.27	2,311	3.05	75,666

According to 1991 Census of India, women constitute 48.14% of the Indian population but only 32.41% of women are literate. Sexwise distribution of the students at IGNOU (See Table 3 : Genderwise Enrolment of Students - 1986-87 to 1992-93) also reveals that the proportion of male students is much higher than female students.

TABLE 3

YEARWISE/GENDERWISE ENROLMENT OF STUDENTS

(1986-87 to 1992-93)

Year	Male		Female		Total
	Number	Percentage	Number	Percentage	
1986-87	4,146	94.64	235	5.36	4,381
1987-88	12,137	72.20	4,674	27.80	16,811
1988-89	35,130	83.00	7,194	17.00	42,324
1989-90	44,266	91.68	4,015	8.32	48,281
1990-91	45,322	86.53	7,054	13.47	52,376
1991-92	53,421	85.64	8,954	14.36	62,375
1992-93	55,776	73.71	19,890	26.29	75,666

The precentage of women also differs according to types of courses viz. liberal education, continuing education and professional courses (See Table 4 : Yearwise and Coursewise Gender Profile of IGNOU Students). No doubt, there is a steady increase in their enrolment every subsequent year but the reason for their disproportionate enrolment is the low literacy rate among women due to social and traditional discrimination in the Indian society.

TABLE 4
COURSEWISE/YEARWISE GENDER PROFILE OF IGNOU STUDENTS. (1990-91, 1991-92, 1992-93)

Course	Year	Male Number	Male %	Female Number	Female %	Total
BPP	1990-91	9,057	80.6	2,180	19.4	11,237
	1991-92	6,031	78.7	1,633	21.3	7,664
	1992-93	9.050	76.2	2,822	23.8	11,872
BDP	1990-91	10,714	77.7	3,075	22.3	13,789
	1991-92	10,991	72.8	4,113	27.2	15,104
	1992-93	16,417	69.7	7,150	30.3	23,567
BLS	1990-91	1,345	71.8	527	28.2	1,872
	1991-92	837	57.3	624	42.7	1,461
	1992-93	814	55.3	659	44.7	1,473
CFN	1990-91	1,147	39.3	1,722	60.7	2,919
	1991-92	1,363	24.1	4,292	75.9	5,655
	1992-93	1,086	18.2	4,871	81.8	5,957
DCE	1990-91	100	100	-	-	100
	1991-92	262	56.00	206	44.0	468
	1992-93	321	55.9	253	44.1	574
DCO	1990-91	436	90.1	48	9.9	484
	1991-92	534	86.0	87	14.0	621
	1992-93	731	85.69	122	14.31	853
DDE	1990-91	608	73.7	217	26.3	825
	1991-92	304	62.8	180	37.2	484
	1992-93	303	62.47	182	37.53	485
DIM/	1990-91	11,240	94.8	605	5.2	11,845
SDM	1991-92	11,567	93.0	836	7.0	12,403
	1992-93	24,073	92.3	2,022	7.7	26,095
DHE	1991-92	617	71.6	245	28.4	862
	1992-93	593	63.2	345	36.8	938
DRD	1991-92	2,355	78.6	643	21.4	2,998
	1992-93	1,738	73.3	632	26.7	2,370
MADE	1990-91	158	84.0	30	15.0	188
DCH	1991-92	164	77.0	49	23.0	213
CIG	1992-93	328	30.3	753	69.7	1,081

Though undergraduate courses leading to B.A. and B. Com. degrees are conducted by all the conventional universities and correspondence directorates, it is found that 46.83% students have opted for these traditional, liberal education courses in 1992-93 compared to professional courses. Management courses are heavily dominated by male students. Hardly 7.7% of women have been enrolled for Management Programmes in 1992-93. The proportion of women enrolment is the highest in Certificate in Food and Nutrition (81.8%), Certificate in Guidance (69.66%), Diploma in Creative Writing in English (44.08%) and Bachelor in Library and Information Science (44.7%). But it is interesting to note that Certificate Course in Food and Nutrition primarily meant for women has attracted 18.8% male students. Women students perhaps do not take education as a means of enhancement of their social status. Education for them is only an added attainment. Hence, their concentrations in stereotyped courses meant for women the home-maker or courses of a general nature. But, they should look forward to opportunities in the field of management and entrepreneurship, science and technology, computers etc. so as to be equal partners in the society. Thus it is essential for IGNOU to develop more management and entrepreneurial courses for women through distance teaching.

In the Indian situation, when it comes to introduction of more courses for women, may it be through adult, literacy, continuing, life-long and distance education or professional, vocational, technical and career education, educationists think of producing only sex-stereotyping, elementary courses such as general literacy programmes, agricultural extension programmes and family health programmes like health and hygiene, sanitation, family planning, food and nutrition, maternity and childcare for rural and tribal women. It is very common for universities to start traditional domestic or home science courses. There are many private and government organisations for women which have handicrafts and cottage crafts programmes like sewing, knitting, embroidery and needle work, tailoring, fabric painting, flower arrangement, canework, potteries and so on. Some associations conduct catering programmes like cookery for various cuisines, baking, food processing and preservation, making squashes, pickles and jam. In urban regions, it is common to have secretarial and commercial practice, interior decoration, nursing, beauty courses for facials and cosmetology etc.

Every country, whether developed or developing, has reviewed its approach to equality of access to education for women but the circumstances and emphasies differ according to its economic, social and political situation and traditional, historical and cultural biases. In order to encourage equal participation of men and women, it is essential for IGNOU not to develop sex-stereotyped courses under the brand of women's education, but play an interventionist role by producing multi-disciplinary courses pertaining to engineering, science and technology, business management, computer science and informatics, electronics, and so on for professional development of both men and women. It is noteworthy to mention here that the IGNOU has already taken measures for developing a few such courses.

The staff of IGNOU can be broadly grouped into two categories:

1. Regular Staff and
2. Contractual Staff.

As the literal meanings of the terms suggest, regular staff are those who are appointed through proper recruitment procedure whereas contractual staff are selected to do specific time-bound jobs either on full-time or part-time basis.

The gender disproportion is conspicuous in the staff profile too (See Table 5 : Gender Profile of IGNOU Staff). The overall involvement of women's participation is less than 22%. The percentage of women employed as regular and contractual staff is 26.6% and 10.79% respectively.

It is clear from Table 5 that except for regular academic staff where male and female percentages are 62.03% and 37.97% respectively, in all the other categories of the regular and contractual staff, the percentage ranges between 0% to 23.83%. The reason

TABLE 5

GENDER PROFILE OF IGNOU STAFF

Category		Male Number	Male %	Female Number	Female %	Total
I	**REGULAR STAFF :-**					
A	*VC + PVCs*	4	100.00	-	-	1 + 3
B	*Officers*	24	100.00	-	-	24 *
	Total	28	100	-	-	28
C	*Teachers :-*					
i)	Professors	21	91.30	2	8.70	23
ii)	Readers	26	81.25	6	18.75	32
iii)	Lecturers	51	49.51	52	50.49	103 @
	Total	98	62.03	60	37.97	158
D	*Other Academic Staff*					
i)	Regional Drectors	13	100.00	-	-	13
ii)	Assistant Reg. Directors/Lecturers	41	73.21	15	26.79	56
	Total	54	78.26	15	21.74	69
E	*Technical/Professional Staff*					
i)	Group A	21	72.41	8	27.59	29
ii)	Group B	23	85.18	4	14.82	27
iii)	Group C	138	86.25	22	13.75	160
	Total	182	84.26	34	15.74	216
F	*Administrative Staff*					
i)	Group A	44	97.77	1	2.23	45
ii)	Group B	66	89.18	8	10.82	74
iii)	Group C	296	71.49	118	28.51	414
	Total	406	76.17	127	23.83	533
II	**CONTRACTUAL STAFF :-**					
A	*Consultants*	3	75.00	1	25.00	4
B	*Co-ordinators*	116	91.47	11	8.53	129
C	*UGC/GOI Staff*	2 + 1	50.00	3	50.00	6
		124	89.2	15	10.79	139
	Total	892	78.04	251	21.96	1143

* Includes 10 Professors.

@ Includes lecturers posted at Regional Centres.

can be attributed to low literacy rate among women. Again, according to the UGC report, only 30% of female candidates are enrolled in graduate and postgraduate courses out of which, a few drop out of the courses without appearing for examination or getting the degree.

It is obvious that the gender disproportion in the enrolment of students and staff in India in general and at IGNOU in particular is due to the social and cultural bias and rigid assignment of roles for both sexes in Indian society. It may not be construed that by describing the situation of students and staff at IGNOU, the author is critical of the institution. The status of women is caught up in the quagmire of social prejudices leading to the rejection of women, which in turn leads to low literacy rates and paucity of personnel from among women. It is essential to break this tradition and improve women's paricipation rates in education as well as employment. This can be possible only by raising literacy rates of women and giving them equal access to higher education in all areas. No doubt, it seems to be difficult but it is not impossible. Distance education system can fulfil the new socio-economic demands to bring social change. It can be the only viable alternative to lessen the pressure on the formal system of and educate a large number of people by identifying target groups and producing courses of their requirements and choice. Thus, IGNOU faces a great challenge and has an important role to play in translating the dream of providing equitable opportunities to all sections of society, especially to women, into a reality.

REFERENCES

IGNOU (1991). Annual Report : 1990-91. New Delhi : IGNOU.

——— (1992). Annual Report : 1991-92. New Delhi : IGNOU.

——— (1993). Annual Report : 1992-93. New Delhi : IGNOU.

IGNOU Status Report: May 1989. Prepared by Planning and Development Division. New Delhi: IGNOU (Mimeographed).

India, Ministry of Human Resource Development (May 1986). *National Policy on Education-1986*. New Delhi: Department of Education.

India, Ministry of Human Resource Development (August 1986). *National Policy on Education 1986: Programme of Action.* New Delhi: Department of Education.

Ogles by K.L. and others (1985). Adult Education for women, in: *The International Encyclopaedia of Education Research and Studies* ed. by Husen, Torsten ad Postlethwaite, T. Neville V.1.p.125-136. Oxford: Pergamon.

Mani, Gomathi ed. (1989). *Women in distance education: Issues and Prospects*, Madras : UNICEF for WIN of ICDE.

WOMEN-FRIENDLY PERSPECTIVES IN DISTANCE EDUCATION: PROBLEMS AND PROSPECTS WITH SPECIAL REFERENCE TO INDIAN CONDITIONS

B.K. KAMALA

Women have many and grave problems, but none that cannot be solved by that magic word: education.

-Swami Vivekananda

Education is an enlightening process. Mere literacy should not be equated with this. Literacy is no doubt a very important instrument in the process. The concept of education was held high by Swami Vivekananda, the leader of the spiritual renaissance of modern India. In his view education is life-building, character making assimilation of ideas. And, knowledge is 'discovering' or 'unveiling' (Avinasilingam, 1985).

Denying such a noble gift to anyone is unethical. But in history inequalities existed and injustices were heaped on some sections of society based on birth, colour or sex. Women were one such unfortunate section who were deprived of education among other social experiences.

In the earliest times, the Vedic period, women had a respectable place. Gargi and Maitreyi, for instance, were mentioned among the 'rishis' - the sages of that age. They fearlessly participated in public debates on the essence of the Vedas. Women had, however, received a setback in the medieval period and the down-sliding continued till about the middle of the nineteenth century. This was the time when prominent reformist movements started in India. The work and teachings of such great personalities as Raja Ram Mohan Roy, Keshav Chandra Sen, Ishwar Chandra Vidyasagar and Swami Vivekananda made invaluable contributions to the uplift and alleviation of sufferings of women. Swami Vivekananda declared : if the women are raised, their children will by their noble actions glorify the name of the country; then will culture, knowledge, power and devotion awaken in the country (Avinasilingam, 1985).

Poet Rabindranath Tagore and Mahatma Gandhi spared no efforts for an awakening among women. The Mahatma's teachings helped raising the marriage age as a result of which there was progress in the field of education among women (Lahkar, 1987). Inspired by these changes other social workers took up the cause. In the south of the country, for instance, Smt. Durgabai Deshmukh worked for the welfare and education of women.

In free India the different five-year plans helped to spread literacy among women. As late as in the 1980's the Executive Secretary of ESCAP stressed that the future of development and society lies in the future of women, equally with men. Women's problems cannot be treated as secondary issues (Gupta, 1986).

Distance Education and Women

Uplift of women is one of the objectives of education in free India. Colleges and institutions are established exclusively for them in all important towns. Special provisions also exist for them to study graduate courses. All these are available in the formal stream of education.

In the context of women lagging much behind men and a majority of them having already missed the opportunity, the formal method of education is not adequate to compensate for the losses. New methods need to be evolved for "reaching out to the society in its totality by imaginative non-formal educational measures" (Scarlet, 1986). Such a need appears to have been variously felt before as a result of which correspondence and distance education have gradually emerged on the scene. This trend is, however, of recent origin. Though some correspondence courses have been started by various formal universities, the first full-fledged open university took shape only in 1982 in Andhra Pradesh followed by the Indira Gandhi National Open University (IGNOU) which is now the apex body for the open system of learning. Four other open universities also emerged in the states.

Problems and Perspectives

These universities include women as one of the several beneficiary groups to avail themselves of the opportunities of higher learning provided by them (Prasad, 1992). It is however a matter of concern for women that they are not accorded any special status in the objectives incorporated in the mandates of these universities.

As a result of this approach women's enrolment in these institutions has been only marginal. Their problems were not studies with a view to paying special attention to solve them. The results of a study conducted at Dr. Ambedkar Open University (Evaluation Centre) affirms this view. Enrolment of women candidates in the undergraduate courses in the year 1983-84 was 15 per cent out of a total 6,231. It rose to 29 per cent (in a total 19,271) by 1986-87 and remained around that level without further increase (1989-90 : 31% in 16,402; 1991-92 : 27% in 32,423).

A large number of the women learners are housewives. Their figures for various academic years are 1983-84 : 68%; 1986-87 : 87%; 1989-90 : 87%; 1991-92 : 85.3%. The remaining are either teachers, employed in other establishments or others including a few unemployed unmarried women. Over three-fourths of the entire group are between 16 and 25 years of age. The profile reveals that a great majority of women are overburdened discharging responsibilities at home and/or at the work place. In Indian conditions where males do not share any responsibility at home the plight of these women learners is anybody's guess. But nothing is done yet to reduce this burden or provide extra care and facilities for them.

The relation between family burden and adverse effects on education is more apparent in the findings of another study (Evaluation Centre) of dropouts from courses in the year 1989. Among all the unemployed women who discontinued study, 29 per cent did so due to the reason of 'marriage' and 23 per cent due to 'family problems'. Among the employed 'family problems' and financial problems accounted for 33.7 per cent and 22.8 per cent respectively. It may be noted that family problems emanate from non-cooperation and extra burden at home. But the following results of a study made by the present author (1993) present a different picture of those who are continuing studies and are certainly different from the dropouts (Table 1).

TABLE 1

PROBLEMS EXPRESSED BY WOMEN LEARNERS IN THE 1ST AND 2ND YEAR UNDERGRADUATE COURSE

Problem	Number Expressing the Difficulty			
	1st Year N=45	2nd Year N=30	Total	Percent
ACADEMIC				
Delayed supply of Study material	9	5	14	19.0
Difficulty with Subject/ Exams/Counselling inadequate	7	13	20	27.0
Time inconvenient for employed	3	4	7	9.0
DOMESTIC	1	9	10	13.0
FINANCIAL	2	2	4	5.0
PHYSICAL FACILITIES:				
Transport/Water/ Canteen	-	5	5	7.0
NO PROBLEMS	26	9	35	47.0

In general, academic problems are viewed as more important. Domestic problems come next with only 13 per cent expressing them as an impediment to their studies. The first year learners view the latter as much less important. Physical facilities and financial difficulties are considered to be least significant. Interestingly a large number (47%) do not find any problems in the pursuit of their studies.

The contrasting situation may perhaps be explained by a difference that must exist in the motivation levels of the two categories—those who are 'in the course' and those who 'discontinued'. A second explanation could be that the former represent the typical modest Indian women who are used to bearing hardship without complaining.

The findings on motivation for joining, or the perceived benefits from the courses reveal that knowledge and curiosity to learn is the strongest motive (Evaluation Centre, 1991-92). Forty per cent of the women learner expressed this motive. The second most popular motivation is the desire to be equal with other graduates in the family. The open university opportunity is therefore the best means for realising this aspiration. A good number of women (22%) gave this response.

Gaining 'social status' (14%), prospects of promotion in career (13%) and employment opportunity (11%) rank third, fourth and fifth respectively. In a recent study, by the present author, of the 'goals to achieve' through a distance education course 75 women learners were interviewed. The pattern of responses broadly agrees with the above results (Table-2).

Aiming at obtaining a degree or using distance education as an opportunity for advanced studies is the first goal (71.0%).

The second most important goal is knowledge (47%). The first year learners seem to be a bit more idealistic. A relatively larger number of them value this goal as important. The next goal in the 'direct' category is getting a job or promotion (23 percent). The most important in the 'indirect' category of goals is the use of distance education as the best opportunity by women, housewives or employed persons. Social recognition and philanthrophic or social work rank last with 8% and 7% responses respectively.

TABLE 2
RESPONSES (IN FREQUENCIES AND PERCENTAGES) FOR 'GOALS TO ACHIEVE' BY JOINING DISTANCE EDUCATION COURSES

Problem	Under-graduate Programme			
	1st Year N=45	2nd Year N=30	Total	Per cent
DIRECT				
Knowledge	24	11	35	47.0
Degree/Higher Education	32	21	53	71.0
Job/Promotion	11	6	17	23.0
INDIRECT				
Utilising a good opportunity (for women/ employed)	12	9	21	28.0
Social recognition	3	3	6	8.0
Equip to help self/children/ others	5	-	5	7.0
No specific aim	2	-	2	3.0

Contrary to expectations, for learners, encouragement and inspiration have been coming from family members. Among the employed 31 per cent receive encouragement from friends and 25 per cent from husbands. Unemployed women draw their inspiration, 33 per cent from parents, 32 per cent from husbands and 20 per cent from friends (Evaluation Centre). These findings are in themselves quite encouraging.

Scope for Improvement

Notwithstanding the statistics reported certain difficulties do exist. By correcting them in favour of women better results can be achieved. And women's potential can be utilised in a more gainful way. The corrections relate to two areas : (1) the physical and infrastructural arrangements and (2) the academic component of courses.

(1) Insfrastructure

Study centres are the link between the learners and the university/institution in the process of learning-teaching. The practice of using the accommodation and other material facilities of regular conventional institutions/colleges is defendable on the grounds of financial constraints and economy. But some of the centres lack basic amenities such as canteens, rest and recreation rooms, adequate water supply and toilet facilities. Though few have mentioned them as their problems, these certainly need to be attended to; public transport facilities should be improved to facilitate easy access to study centres. The counselling programmes are arranged on holidays and Sundays. Women mostly depend on husbands/children/brothers for transport to reach the centres. Efforts must be made to run special buses on these days to women's study centres so that they need not depend on others.

Besides, there are difficulties in library accommodation. The libraries at the centres are fairly well-equipped with books and audios/videos. But proper utilisation of these could not be made due to space problems. Generally the study centres are provided with only one hall as permanent accommodation. One room/hall should be provided for the exclusive use of the library.

(2) Academic Component

The courses presently offered by the Distance Education Institutions are a serious hindrance to women's progress. Conventional courses, B.A., B.Sc., B.Com., M.A., etc., have gained a place of prominence. This weakness has been realised by some universities and the need to start purposeful courses such as the following has been felt (Andhra Pradesh Open University : A Critical Profile):

* environment awareness and protection
* population education
* general health and hygiene and
* women's studies.

The list can be extended adding more courses as recommended by the Kothari Commission (Lahkar, 1987):

* home science
* nursing
* education and
* social work.

These changes require a reorientation of the goals of Distance Education:

* Women should be considered as one of the special groups to receive the highest priority in all respects : allocation of resources, designing of courses and monitoring and evaluating the degree to which the goals are achieved.
* The charter of objectives should be modified to clearly state and achieve these goals.
* The orientation must be changed from information-transferring to development and the realisation of potential.

REFERENCES

Avinasilingam, T.S. (ed.), (1985). *Education*. Sri Ramakrishna Math, Madras.

Gupta, A.K. (1986). *Women and Society*. New Delhi: Criterion Publications.

Lahkar, B. (1987). *Development in Women's Education*, Gauhati: Omsons.

Prasad, V.S. (1992). "Dr. B.R. Ambedkar Open University : A Decennial Perspective", *Indian Journal of Open Learning,* Vol.1, No.2, pp.11-17.

Scarlet, E.T. (1986). "Socio-cultural and Attitudinal Factors Affecting the Status of Women". In Amit Kumar Gupta (ed.), *Women and Society.* New Delhi: Criterion Publications.

RESEARCH IDENTIFYING NEED-BASED PROGRAMMES FOR WOMEN

MUKTA PRAHLAD

Introduction

> Women form a third of the world's official labour force but are more vulnerable to unemployment than men. In the agricultural sector, women grow almost half the world's food, but own hardly any land. In many countries (like India) women cannot obtain loans or own property and often are not included in agricultural development projects. At the same time, women perform most of the world's domestic work, which means that many women work a double day. Women provide more health care than all health services combined, yet outnumber men among the world's illiterates, and in almost all countries of the world they have less formal education than men.... Economically, socially and politically women exercise less control and power than men...
>
> (Fagerlind and Saha 1989:167)

This summary of the differences that exist globally between men and women that crystallised at the Nairobi Women's Conference (1985) aptly captures the state of women in India today.

> Women constitute almost 50% of the country's population yet their share of the job market is 27%. Eighty per cent of the unskilled agricultural labourers are women and 97% of all female workers are in the unorganised sector: they work in the fields, they participate in construction work, labour in the factories, work in mines and engage in trade and vending. In

> addition they have the burden of bearing and rearing children, collecting and fetching water, gathering firewood, cooking and cleaning activities which consume much time and energy.... Although women work for longer hours and contribute substantially to the family income, they are not perceived as workers...."
>
> (*Shramshakti,* 1989:1)

The educational status of women is still far from satisfactory. 57% of the country's illiterate population consists of women, and 70% of the children who have not entered school are girls. This low enrolment rate of girls, coupled with a high dropout rate has resulted in the rise in the number of illiterate women in the country from 158.7 million in 1951 to 241.7 million in 1981. Though policy makers have argued for universal education and for using education to create an equal society, educational policies are constrained by the socio-economic conditions of the people, their attitudes and culture. The various literacy programmes have not made any significant impact on literacy levels. If educational reform is to take place "apart from increasing adult literacy, the content of education has to be modified to incorporate new value systems regarding the role of women in the family and community" (*National Perspective Plan for Women,* 1988:74).

Planners have shifted their focus in recent years from equipping women for their traditional roles of housewives and mothers to recognizing their worth as producers, making a major contribution to the family and national income. To make women better able to contribute to national development, it is necessary to provide them ways of improving their employment potential. For this, education is essential. In the National Policy on Education (1986), education is seen as a vehicle for the empowerment of women by seeking to provide for women's equality. According to the *Programme of Action* for the implementation of the National Policy the empowerment of women consists in

- building a positive self-image and self-confidence

- developing the ability to think critically
- building up group cohesion and fostering decision-making
- ensuring equal participation in bringing about social change
- providing the means for economic independence

The programme entails elementary education for girls, adult education for girls in the age group of 15-35; increased access for women to vocational and professional training programmes and the review of existing educational activities to ensure that they make a substantial contribution towards women's equality.

However, it is estimated that at the current rate of provision and through conventional literacy and development programmes, female literacy cannot be reached in the country for another nine decades i.e. for almost another century. If we are to accelerate the process of providing literacy and educational opportunities to our women, we have to look for systems and approaches where the outreach is greater. Distance education programmes can reach out to a larger number than conventional programmes and have the added advantage of providing opportunities to those women who fall outside the purview of conventional programmes. Furthermore, they can reach these women without displacing them from their homes and workplace and can therefore be psychologically more acceptable to them and their families.

Distance education, comparatively speaking, is still in its infancy and little sustained research has been done on its potential for redressing the educational imbalance in our country, particularly in its relevance for the education of women. In this chapter an attempt is made to identify the thrust areas where distance education can reach out to women. It is hypothesized that for any programme to be meaningful it must be based on an identification of the needs of the target population. The aim here is to identify the needs of women learners and on that basis examine the validity of the courses offered for women in the socio-cultural milieu in which they operate, and identify ways of reaching out to them.

The paper is divided into three parts. In the first part the role of education in national development, specifically the education of women is discussed. The second part of the paper reviews the status of women in India today and from that seeks to identify the special needs of women as a target group. The third part explores the potential of the distance mode of education for reaching out to women, reviews research done on provision for women's education through the distance mode and seeks to identify potential areas for research which can make the mode truly meaningful for meeting women on their own ground.

Education of Women and National Development

Philosophers and social scientists have long been concerned with the role that education plays in the development process. Some policy makers and political thinkers have seen technological advancement as most important, while others have focused on social well-being. The key factor that has affected both technological advancement and socio-economic development is education.

While schooling and education were earlier viewed as elitist and in individual rather than societal terms, formal education is now perceived as playing a more direct and causal role in economic development and is being utilized as a contributory factor to rapid industrialization and as 'a key change agent for moving societies along the development continuum' (Fagerlind and Saha, 1989:40).

Investment in education has been justified by the following assumptions :

1. An educated population contributes to the socio-economic development of the society as a whole. Rapidly changing technologies and the changing face of the world's economy and political systems require a new flexibility and adaptibility by societies and individuals. Education is seen as an essential component for an adaptable and flexible population.
2. The most efficient path to the national development of any society lies in the improvement of its population, its human capital. Education contributes to the well-being of this

human capital, the individuals within society. It not only improves the individual choices available to men, but an educated population provides the kind of labour force necessary for economic growth and industrial development. Illiteracy and lack of education lead to wastage of human talent potentially available for the benefit of society. Human capital theorists argue that for economic growth there must be technological advancement which will lead to greater production. They argue, however, that the utilization of human resources is equally important for the use of technology. Education can improve the production capacity of a population.

3. In order for a society to become modern (i.e., to develop economically and socially) it must be composed of a modern population, with a set of modern beliefs and values about work, the quality of life and the desirability of controlling one's environment. According to the modernization theory there are five variables in the process of modernization and there is a causal link between them. Modernizing *institutions* leads to modernization of *values*, this leads to modernization of *behaviour* which in turn, leads to modernization of *society*. Modernization of society leads ultimately to *economic development.*

To modernize is to develop and a society cannot hope to develop until its population holds modern values. The creation of modern values can be the result of human planning and social institutions like the family, school and workplace can help influence their emergence.

> ... it is impossible for a state to move into the twentieth century if its people continue to live in an earlier era. A modern nation needs participating citizens, men and women who take an active interest in public affairs and who exercise their rights and perform their duties as members of a community larger than that of the kinship network and the immediate geographical

> locality (Inkeles and Smith 1974:3).

Education is considered the most important agent for changing a traditional society into a modern one.

> In the Indian context, the concept of national development goes far beyond economic growth; it is concerned equally with the creation of a self-confident individual, with a strong commitment to democratic values, concerned with the creation of a nation united in purpose... In a society which has chosen the democratic rather than the totalitarian path of development, education has to be the mainstay of all national endeavours (*Challenge of Education* 1985:4).

Women are critical inputs for national development, yet in all three dimensions of national development, economy, modernization and quality of life, and political participation women lag far behind men.

Planners have seen education as the key factor which can contribute to changing the national fabric, on the assumption that investment in human capital promotes political and economic growth. Some of the goals set for education by our *National Policy of Education* (1985) are *to modernise the nation*: "to transform a static society into one vibrant with a commitment to development and change" (Foreword). *To improve the quality of life*: "building a dynamic, vibrant and cohesive nation, capable of providing its people with the wherewithal for creating a better, fuller and more purposeful life" (para 1.2). *To develop human capital:* "the development of human resource is the main function of education" (para 1.4).

It is therefore through education that the government seeks to provide women their constitutional rights. While 75% of the women of the country remain illiterate, they have little chance of entering the organised labour sector and their contribution to the national economy and national development will remain invisible. If economic independence is linked with development, education can be a vital means of empowering women. However, despite the high investment in education, women as a group have not benefited proportionally.

Access to education for women has been limited because of institutional factors within the society and family which have contrived to exclude the majority of women from participating in educational opportunities. In addition, modern sector jobs requiring education pose a conflict between women's roles within the family and outside employment. Women are caught in a vicious circle. On the one hand they are late starters in the race for education, on the other, when access to education is granted, the opportunity cost of fully utilizing the benefits of education rises. (Shields, 1987 in Psacharapoulos, 121). While the participation of men in the labour force is taken for granted after they complete education, this generalisation cannot be made about women. Women's decisions to enter the workforce are affected by a range of socio-economic factors. Social attitudes about the propriety of women working and the jobs suitable for women, and women's own image of themselves as workers determine the nature of work sought by women. In addition, because of the childbearing role of women, their non-participation in the workforce is socially acceptable, even recommended.

Shields (1987) identifies three interrelated factors which lead to a positive relationship between the level of education and female employment. He says education induces women to seek employment by increasing the following:

a) the desire to work for psychological or economic satisfaction.
b) a woman's productivity in the labour market relative to home if cheap surrogate care is available.
c) the probability of finding employment as it increases the range of employment opportunities.

The three factors that Shields has identified as leading to a positive relationship between education and employment are also the factors that militate against the education of women.

Evidence from cumulative research has shown that a combination of socio-economic factors is responsible for inequalities not only in the labour market but also in education. Also, social attitudes about the status and role of women shape women's own image of themselves as workers. Women live in a culture which affords them a low status. Women work in difficult and low paid jobs with long hours. In addition they carry the burden of domestic chores. Men get better paid jobs and better opportunities for training in vocational skills. As the education of women more closely approximates to that of men, so too will their participation in the workforce. Providing girls with access to schools is only the beginning. If attrition rates are to be reduced, conditions need to be provided so that girls remain in school and ultimately have an equal opportunity to participate in productive activity.

It is in this context that we shall look at the status of women in India in the next part of the paper. This will enable us to identify the thrust areas for the education of women. It is argued that these priority areas for the education of women are also the potential areas for research on the education of women through the distance mode.

The Educational Status of Women in India Today

The National Perspective Plan for Women (1988) views women "not as the weaker segment of society or as passive beneficiaries of the development process, but as a source of unique strength for reaching goals." Our women, however, live in a society which affords them a low status. Some areas where the inequalities between men and women are clear are education and literacy, employment prospects and social benefits. Some of the research findings on the status of Indian women are cited below. These are based on statistics provided by the Census of India and from other research done on Indian women today.

Literacy and Education

While the total literacy rate in the country went up from 29.4% in 1971 to 36% in 1981, women as a group do not seem to have benefited much from the literacy drive. In 1981, women still constituted 75% of the illiterate population in India, with an even higher illiteracy rate obtaining in rural areas (82%). Even in the urban areas 52% of the women were illiterate. In some states like Uttar Pradesh and Madhya Pradesh the literacy figure for women was as low as 15% and in Rajasthan 11.42% (*Literacy Digest*, 1988).

Furthermore, women belonging to SC/ST groups living in rural areas seemed to be greatly handicapped where literacy is concerned, as shown in the table below (from Dandekar, 1990:159).

Literacy (%) in Rural Areas (1981)

	Non-SC	SC
Male	46.14	27.91
Female	21.68	8.44

Of the literate population, the majority of literate women are in urban areas, and very few women in rural areas (1.68%) reach the matriculation level (Dandekar 1990:161), as shown in the table below:

Male/Female Educational Level [(%) in 1981]

	Primary & Middle		Matriculation and Above	
	Male	Female	Male	Female
Total	25.82	14.46	11.95	4.51
Rural	23.75	10.85	7.21	1.68
Urban	32.10	26.43	26.37	13.89

In 1981, men holding degrees and diplomas constituted 5.1% of the total literate population. Non-technical degree, diploma and postgraduate degree holders constitued 80% of all degree holders.

This means that only 20% of all the degree holders in the country have technical degrees. Among technical degree holders, women are fairly well-represented in the medical profession but have a low representation in engineering and technology. There is little provision for technical courses in rural areas, so the concentration of women holding technical degrees is in urban areas.

Figures, however, show that there has been an increase in the number of women going in for higher education and also for research and postgraduate courses. There is a trend for more women to enrol for research and postgraduate courses than for diploma/certificate courses (Gomathi Mani, 1988:13). Gomathi Mani cites the following figures to show the rise in enrolment from 1981-82 to 1985-86.

Enrolment of Women in Higher Education

	1981-82	1985-86	% increase
Graduate Courses	27.7%	29.6%	1.9%
Postgraduate Courses	26.6%	30.9%	2.3%
Research Programmes	27.7%	32.3%	4.6%
Diploma/Certificate Courses	21.5%	23.3%	1.8%

Gender inequalities are also manifested in the educational and employment opportunities for women.

Educational Opportunities

In our society the benefits of educating a girl are seen to pass on to her in-laws and so investment in the education of a girl is considered a loss for the family, while educating boys is considered a gain. Secondly, when there are economic constraints on education, educating a son is always given preference to educating a daughter, since a son is seen to have better employment prospects than a daughter. Thirdly, especially among the rural poor, the fact that the mother is employed prevents the daughter from having access to education as she has to remain at home to cook, fetch water and firewood, and care for younger siblings.

Educational opportunities are often restricted for women by men because men see women's education as a threat to their control over women's lives. Government provision for more opportunities for girls to receive education has perhaps to be accompanied by awareness raising programmes for village adults to enable them to see better the need for, and benefits of, educating women.

Vocational Training

Men are given precedence over women in vocational training programmes, and in the case of jobs which are considered typically female occupations, there are few vocational training programmes available. Women consequently have little access to better tools or to technological advances. The introduction of new technology requires new skills. Since women do not have access to training facilities, they cannot acquire new skills and are forced to join the ranks of casual and marginal workers.

Though it is estimated that 30% of households are headed by women, especially among the poor, as a result of death, migration, desertion or illness of the husbands, social security schemes do not recognise women as heads. In women-headed households women take on the dual role of breadwinner and home-maker. Lack of better employment opportunities prevents women from improving their living conditions. Lack of civic amenities, social and community facilities and essential services lead to poor living conditions. Poor living conditions ; arduous domestic chores, malnutrition and repeated pregnancies affect their health. The education of women is one important way of improving the quality of their life and of increasing their employment potential.

How Education Can Help?

It has been reported that 6.6% of girls in the 10-14 age group are married. Education is seen to relate negatively with age at marriage.

With education, even with mere literacy, women's age at marriage rises as is shown in the table below:

Urban Women's Age at Marriage

Education Level	Age
Illiterate	16.7
Primary School	17.4
Below matriculation	18.1
Matriculation	19.8
Graduation	21.7

These are figures pertaining to urban women. In rural areas the average age at marriage is much lower. Since a large number cf rural women are illiterate it is important to promote their education to push their age at marriage to at least 19 years. The average rural woman gets pregnant 6-8 times, spends about 16 years in pregnancy and lactation, gives birth to more than six children of whom four survive (*Shramshakti*, 1989).

Literacy has been found to correlate negatively with the fertility rate/crude birth rate and infant mortality rate. Educating a woman can help her improve her health and that of her family. Since literacy has a positive correlation with employment, it can also improve a woman's employment potential. An increase in employment potential will promote a higher income level and a consequent improvement in the standard of living. Adult literacy and education programmes can reach out to this new target group: adult rural women.

Inkeles and Smith (1974) report the findings of a study conducted in six developing countries including India, on the factors that contributed most to the process of modernisation. The three key factors that they identified as having a modernizing effect on the values, beliefs and attitudes of the people were schooling, exposure to media, and work experience.

How the Distance Mode can Help Adult Rural Women

The distance mode of education is a system which is considered especially suitable for reaching out to the adult who cannot, or will not, study through the conventional face-to-face mode. Women, particularly adult rural women, have already been identified as a potential target group whom the distance mode can reach. While conventional learning programmes are perceived as unrelated to the needs of this special group, they are also psychologically unacceptable to them because of the tacit assumption underlying conventional programmes that illiteracy is tantamount to ignorance. On the other hand, a programme which takes note of experiential learning, of the fact that most rural folk learn their trade through apprenticeship not formal training, and which accepts the learner for what she knows, and is prepared to take her from where she is to the targeted goal will be more acceptable to rural woman.

Secondly, the distance mode has the potential to make a wide and constructive use of technology, particularly the communication media and can therefore have greater impact as it can provide education that synthesizes the cognitive and affective functions of education: it can effectively provide knowledge and change attitudes. Statistics show that in rural areas fewer girls enrol at the primary school level and of those who enrol, a higher percentage drop out on attaining puberty. Some of the reasons cited for this phenomenon of low enrolment and high attrition rates are

a) schools are inaccessible and far from their homes;
b) there is a shortage of women teachers and parents are reluctant to send girls to schools where there are no women teachers;
c) on attaining puberty, girls are kept at home either to help look after siblings, or are married;
d) especially among the rural poor, young girls are drawn in as agricultural labour, to work in the fields. Economic pressures become more real and immediate for them than the perceived benefits of literacy and schooling;

e) furthermore, the school curricula are perceived as not being related to these young women's needs and they drop out;
f) young girls, especially the daughters of mothers who work, have to do domestic chores and fetch water, which leaves little time for them to attend school.

The government, in combating these factors, has made attempts at creating awareness about the benefits of educating the girl child, has also taken steps to make schools more accessible i.e. within a radius of 2-5 kilometres of the students' homes. Attempts at making school curricula more relevant to the actual needs of these young women are also being made.

As stated earlier, a two-pronged attack on illiteracy has to be made. Through conventional education basic literacy and numeracy, at least till the primary level, has to be provided. But to combat the high dropout rate and also to provide education to the already large number of adult women who cannot be reached through conventional school programmes, the distance mode seems a powerful alternative. The distance mode is seen as complementary to conventional school education as it reaches out to a target population outside the purview of conventional education.

The advantages of the distance mode seem to lie in its flexibility and in the fact that it can take learning to the women's homes and to their work places. Since it does not displace them from their day-to-day activities, it will not only be psychologically more acceptable to them and their families but it can help them study/learn in groups in their own homes where they can still take care of their children. Such group learning programmes, when supported by the media, (which is a powerful instrument for changing attitudes) can reduce the requirement of trained teachers which rigid school systems demand. The available resources of educated women can be channelled into part-time programmes. Part-time programmes are again more practical. It has been claimed that flexibility is the hallmark of the distance education mode. This flexibility can be utilised in making the learning programmes synchronise with the agricultural calendar, leaving women to work in the fields during peak periods and providing more intensive learning during comparatively slack periods. Another way in which flexibility can be built in is by changing the contact time to timings convenient to rural women. Since most adult education programmes are not necessarily linked with certification, the actual programmes can be more need-based and targeted at the real needs of rural women rather than providing a replication of conventional programmes. Vocational skills can also be provided for special groups through a more open system of learning. Such programmes, it is hoped, will not only draw women into the fold, but keep them within it. The distance mode, it is felt, can more easily realise some of the recommendations of the National Perspective Plan, listed below:

- generate awareness about the necessity of educating girls and women (through wide use of the media which does not require any literacy);
- making school timings more flexible and suited to local conditions and to the needs of the working girls;
- utilising local talent to recruit women teachers especially in rural and tribal areas (since local talent is scarce, it is felt that the distance mode can reach out to more people than conventional schools can);
- providing non-formal education which, in addition to providing literacy, will focus on skill development and building up a positive self-image among women;
- providing vocational training along with basic literacy increase occupational opportunities and may be more attractive to women from weaker sections;
- a multiple entry system. This is possible particularly through the distance mode, which does not have stringent requirements of entry qualifications. Self-study programmes, particularly when basic literacy has been reached will enable more women to learn without attending school;
- the use of the communication media especially more skill training to illiterate women.

Research on Women Learners Studying through the Distance Mode

There is a paucity of research reported on the education/training of women through the distance mode. The research that has been done is sporadic and done by individuals rather than agencies or institutions offering courses through the distance mode. The limited research that has been conducted on women learners in distance education has focused on enrolment rates and enrolment patterns of women learners and some anecdotal findings are also given about the problems faced by women learners. Some of their findings are reported below.

Enrolment of Women in Distance Education Programmes

At present, the courses available through the distance mode are conventional undergraduate and postgraduate programmes of traditional universities. Research studies have therefore been restricted to university courses. However, some of the findings reported have implications for further research and merit some discussion. Gomathi Mani and Rogers (1988) report the following enrolment pattern of women in courses offered through the distance mode vis-a-vis the conventional face to face mode.

Enrolment of Women (%)

Level	Correspondence courses	Conventional courses
Graduate (including LLB.)	34.3%	29.6%
B.Ed.	47.5%	N.A.
Postgraduate (including M.Ed.)	33.9%	30.9%
Diploma/Certificate Courses (Undergraduate + Postgraduate)	13.4%	23.3%
Foundation/Preparation Courses	25.8%	N.A.

In the same paper they also cite the statewise enrolment of women on distance learning programmes. They point out that not all states have courses through the distance mode. Therefore in some geographical areas women learners do not have access to the distance mode of study.

Statewise Enrolment of Women (%) on College/ Correspondence Courses

State	College(%)	Correspondence Courses (%)
Uttar Pradesh	21.1%	40.0%
Bihar	14.5%	32.1%
Rajasthan	21.8%	30.5%
Tamil Nadu	35.8%	32.3%
Karnataka	26.4%	27.9%
Delhi	42.4%	44.9%

Also significant is the fact that in states like Uttar Pradesh, Bihar and Rajasthan where the enrolment of women on face-to-face courses is low (reflecting perhaps the social constraints on women attending college courses) the enrolment through the distance mode is high (as women can study at home without their other roles being disturbed).

As opposed to this in more "progressive" states like Tamil Nadu, Karnataka and Delhi, the enrolment rate through either mode is more or less equal. This seems to point to the fact that when provision is made for women to study, they do take up studies especially if it helps them overcome factors that inhibit their participation in face-to-face educational programmes. This is again borne out by the enrolment figures from Maharashtra. SNDT University offers courses exclusively for women, also through the distance mode. Without including enrolment figures for SNDT

University the enrolment figure for women studying through the distance mode in Maharashtra is 39.9%. On inclusion of the SNDT enrolment figures, the state percentage rises to 59.4%, i.e. almost two-thirds of all distance learners in the state are women. If this is the case with conventional university courses, there are indications that special vocational training programmes for women would be equally popular.

Gomathi Mani and Rogers provide some more interesting data. Statistics for the academic year 1986-87 show that more women (32.9%) study through the distance mode than through conventional courses (29.6%). These figures compare favourably with the enrolment figures reported in Faith (1988) for women studying in some distance teaching universities in the West.

University	Women Learners (%)
Fern Universitat	25%
Turkish Open University	33%
Swedish Open University	44%

Another study (Prummer and Rossie, 1988) of women studying at Fern Universitat shows that the enrolment of women at this Open University is *lower* than their enrolment in some of the traditional universities in Germany (40%). These figures show that the enrolment of women on courses through the distance mode in some developed countries is different from that in India (32.9% in the distance mode vs. 29.6% in conventional universities).

It has been claimed that distance education programmes are particularly suited to the needs of women, but Prummer and Rossie (1988) ascribe the following reasons for the low enrolment of women at Fern Universitat: the range of subjects available to women is limited and the distance education mode puts more pressure on women than men as they have to take care of their families in addition to studying and sometimes holding a job. Since domestic and family help is more easily available to Indian women, this apparently is not a problem for them. But it is a potential area for wider research on enrolment patterns of women distance learners and reasons for the disparity of female participation in university education through the distance mode.

Enrolment Patterns in different Courses

Gomathi Mani and Rogers (1988) provide some data on faculty-wise enrolment of women on programmes offered through the distance mode and through conventional university programmes.

Facultywise Enrolment of Women
(% of Women of All Students Enrolled)

Faculties	Distance Mode (%)	Conventional Mode(%)
Arts	39.1	40.4
Commerce	26.9	19.1
Education	42.7	49.0
Science	23.6	30.5
Engineering and Technology	4.7	5.9
Law	6.5	8.1
Others	42.4	39.5

These figures show that there is no significant difference in the preferences of women studying through the distance mode to those studying through the face-to-face mode. Education courses (teachers training courses primarily) have the highest enrolment followed by Arts courses. This reflects the fact that these are considered women's areas and that the teaching profession is considered "safe" and respectable for women to follow. Enrolment in engineering courses is low not only because of the comparative non-availability of such courses through the distance mode but also because these are considered more suitable for men. Even through the conventional mode, enrolment of women on engineering courses is only marginally higher.

The lack of availability of courses specially suited to women's interests or jobs commonly held by women (except teaching) is reflected in the narrow range of courses offered. Also, these courses are replications of conventional courses run by conventional universities. They are accessible primarily to urban women who have a higher educational level than rural women. There is potential for linking new programmes with organisations other than conventional universities. Such programmes, if organised and offered with the cooperation of factories, labour unions, voluntary agencies and other local agencies, would be need-based in the larger sense as they could be made to serve the needs of the local community.

On the basis of educational attainment and employment potential, we can divide women learners into two distinct groups — urban and rural. If programmes are to cater to the needs of women we must have provision for two distinct types of programmes. This is another potential area for research in distance education for women. An analysis of the needs of a potential target group is a prerequisite for making the course responsive to the actual and perceived needs of the target group.

The studies conducted on women learners focus only on their enrolment. They do not indicate how many actually complete the course and whether more women drop out from courses than men. Also what are the factors that contribute to their dropping out and are they the same as those that apply to men? Enrolment figures which are not backed up by attrition rates would give an unrealistic picture of the actual situation.

Even among women learners themselves we can analyse the situation more closely. How many rural women have access to conventional programmes? Do rural women who enrol for courses have a higher dropout rate than urban women? Do the same factors contribute to their staying on a course or dropping out as for urban women? Do we have any facts or figures on these? Without sufficient data about current enrolment patterns and without it being linked with retention rates, our understanding of the phenomenon is incomplete.

Research on the potential of distance education for women could be conducted under three broad heads:

- Women as distance learners
- Programme development and provision for women learners
- Administration of courses for women learners

The special topics/aspects to be researched under each head could be as follows:

1. *Women as Distance Learners*

a. *an identification of the needs* of different target groups, their prejudices and apprehensions as learners.
b. *identification of the priorities* (in terms of areas of study) of potential women learners.
c. *women as learners*: their study conditions, preferred study modes, learning strategies and styles.
d. *problems faced* by women as distance learners. These problems can relate to
   - coping with the demands of a course, which could have implications for course content
   - coping with the demands of studying along with work and home responsibilities, which would have implications for counselling and other support strategies for women learners.
   - problems in utilising support facilities provided by the supporting organisations. This could focus on women learners' use of study centres, tutoring facilities and other support mechanisms provided by individual institutions.

withdrawal/attrition rates: An identification of the problems faced by women learners would be more significicnt, if studied alongwith completion and attrition rates i.e. how do the problems faced by women prevent them from staying on the course? Alternatively, those who successfully complete a course can be asked to give the "coping strategies" they have evolved and which can help other women.

2. *Programme Development and Provision for Women Learners*

In order to focus on improving the relevance and efficacy of courses provided for women, research would need to focus on the following:

a. *needs assessment*: this would be a broader analysis of needs as it would focus not only on the needs of the learners as individuals but would include societal needs and the priorities of employers.
b. *analysis of resources available* for both programme development and provision. This would include a study of the potential of the media, of teachers/course providers, of funds, of community centres/learning centres. These would have to be linked with the priorities of the community where the programmes would be implemented.
c. *selection of objectives*: objectives that match societal and individual learner expectations would have to be identified and spelt out in terms of an analysis of needs and resources available.
d. *organisation of learning activities* and their suitability to learner needs and programme objectives.
e. *programme evaluation*: research into the efficacy of the programmes offered.

3. *Administration of Courses for Women Learners*

The areas that would have to receive attention are:

a. *Organisation* of the course and its implications for administrative facilities to be provided.
b. *Staffing*.
c. *Support structure*, available and planned to increase and sustain participation.
d. *Resources available*, to be generated, and the allocation of resources for optimum use of the facilities planned.

These areas for research would be suitable to all types of women learners, urban or rural, studying university level courses or elsewhere, as such studies will give an added dimension to our understanding of the problem.

However, in the case of rural women where non-formal courses have been identified as the appropriate type of courses, it would be imperative to begin with an identification of their real and perceived needs. In urban areas it may be feasible to have women doing the same jobs as men and therefore aiming at the same kind of education. In rural areas this aim cannot be realised immediately. We have to take rural women through an intermediary step whereby a large number of adult illiterate women are helped to improve the quality of their lives through social awareness programmes, programmes on health and family care and programmes which will foster self-employment or help cope with the travails of self-employment. Potential learners would be the best people to tell us what their problems are. A needs analysis would enable planners to make programmes more realistic and more acceptable to women.

Since we have identified rural women, particularly women working in the unorganised sector, as the main group for distance education programmes to focus on, we cannot provide conventional print-based courses which the learner can study in the privacy of her home. We have to experiment with group learning situations, with minimal literacy requirements to begin with but with experiential learning forming a major component. We have the opportunity to try the potential of the communication media in educating such women, with the help of social workers/local educated women acting as group coordinators. If the distance mode is to effectively reach the grassroot level, experimentation and research on new methods of 'instruction' has to be built in from the very inception of the programmes.

Research on women in the West focuses on gender desparities in education for women as a special group of learners. Research has focused on programmes offered at the university level. In developed societies providing equality to women means providing them opportunities to get the jobs which have traditionally been reserved for men, particularly in the engineering and technology sector. Though this is true of Indian women too, a very small percentage of Indian women would actually qualify for this kind of participation. In our socio-economic situation where the majority of Indian women live below the subsistence level, improving the quality of their lives has a different connotation. We have to chart a different path for research on our women learners. That is the challenge of distance education in our context.

REFERENCES

Bowman Mary Jean and Anderson C. Arnold (1973). "Human capital and economic modernization in historical perspective" Cited in Fagerlind and Saha, 1989.

Challenge of Education: A policy perspective (1985). Ministry of Education. New Delhi: Government of India.

Dandekar, Kumudini (1990). "Progress of Education of Women in India: 1881-1981", *Journal of Indian School of Political Economy*, Vol.2 No.1. Jan-April 1990.

Fagerlind, Ingemar and Saha, Lawrence J. (1989). *Education and National Development: A Comparative Perspective.* Oxford: Pergamon.

Faith, Karlene (ed.) (1988). *Toward New Horizons for Women in Distance Education: International Perspectives.* London: Routledge.

Gomathi Mani (1988). *Women in Distance Education - Issues and Prospects*. ICDE-WIN.

Gomathi Mani and Rogers, Alan (1988). "Indian Women in Distance Education" in Gomathi Mani, 1988.

Inkeles Alex and Smith David H. (1974). *Becoming Modern.* London: Heinemann Education Books.

Mathur, R.S. et al (1988). *Literacy Digest.* Directorate of Adult Education. New Delhi: Ministry of Human Resource Development.

National Perspective Plan for Women 1988-2000 AD (1988).

Report of the Core Group set up by the Department of Women and Child Development. Ministry of Human Resource Development. New Delhi: Government of India.

National Policy on Education (1986). Ministry of Education. New Delhi: Government of India.

Programme of Action (1986). Ministry of Human Resource Development. New Delhi: Government of India.

Von Prummer, Christine and Rossie Ute (1988). "Gender in Distance Education at the Fern Universitat". *Open Learning.* Vol. 3, No.2, June 1988.

Psacharapoulos, George (ed.) (1987). *Economics of Education Research and Studies.* Oxford: Pergamon.

Schuller, Tom and Megarry Jacquetta (eds.) (1979). *World Yearbook 1979: Recurrent Education and Lifelong Learning.* London: Kogan Page.

Shields, N.G. (1987). "Female Labour and Education" in Psacharapoulos 1987.

Shramshakti (1989). Report of the National Commission on Self-employed women and women in the informal sector. Ahmedabad: SEWA.

WOMEN AND THE MANAGEMENT OF FORESTS

SHOBHITA JAIN

Introduction

In this Chapter I make a case for evolving communication channels by preparing a multi-media package on creative and reflective relationship of women with nature and culture. The package will raise awareness about the nature of links between women and the environment, among the Foresters, NGO functionaries, School Teachers and Health Workers, employed and living in the areas adjacent to forests. All these groups are involved in the implementation of the new forest policy of joint forest management (JFM).

At present, there exists a credibility gap between policy makers/implementers and the people among and with whom the policy of JFM is to be implemented. The aim of this multi-media distance education package is to reduce the gap by building a bridge of interaction between the participants (Forest Departments or FDs, NGOs and the Forest Dwellers) in JFM. The concept of JFM is based on the premise that forest-dependent tribal/rural communities, particularly females among them, are going to be the main actors in operationalisation of the new forest policy. In this situation, I find it essential to understand the nature of relationship between women and the environment for developing an approach to securing women's participation in managing forests.

Forest management is at present conceived as the application of scientific and technological principles to conserve forest resources. Such problems as depletion and degradation of forests, owing largely to their uncontrolled exploitation by and for a few, arise despite scientific and rational management. The complexity and diversity of species and their interlinkages defy scientific and technological solutions; only then, forest department personnel become concerned with the management of what people can and cannot do to the forest. Scientific and technological solutions alone prove to be inadequate in dealing with problems occurring at the interface of development (people and society) and the environment (living resources).

As an alternative we have to turn to ecological principles and approaches which are embedded in the values of environmental harmony and *real* socio-economic benefits. The ecological notion of systemic equilibrium is based on the view of humans as just one species among others in the biosphere. It is necessary to educate both the present-day decision-makers (forest department personnel) and the consumer-public (including the communities living in and around forests) about the ecological values of treating humans as part of a larger community of living beings and non-living elements. We need innovative ways of articulating the concepts (enshrined in the World Conservation Strategy) of the value of maintaining ecological processes and life support systems, preserving genetic diversity and ensuring the sustainable utilisation of species and ecosystems.

In this task we can utilise cultural resources of local communities living in and around forests and their empirical knowledge of environmental and technological responses to their survival requirements. Through the mode of distance educational technology of producing a multi-media package, it is possible to handle both the common features of forest management and the cultural plurality of its practice by tribal/rural communities. Traditional knowledge at the command of tribal/rural women and its role in the management of forests is still useful for promoting sustainable resource use. Rooted in the local ecological culture it has the potential of articulating restrained use of diverse forest resources. Those women and men, who live in close proximity to forests and depend on forest resources, develop, over time, the processes of equitable resource allocation and fix priorities for resource use, usually acceptable to the majority of the users. It is worth our while to bring out women's agelong deposit of experience in forest management.

The words 'management of forests' project masculine images. Important roles of women in management of trees are, on the other hand, obscured by their stereotyped roles as housewives. In the wake of the wood energy crisis, foresters and others (like the non-governmental organisations involved in developmental work) have come to recognise the significance of developing alternative, cost-effective energy systems and women's potential for heavy involvement in such forestry-related activities as nursery raising, tree farming, gathering and drying leaves for leaf-meal production. But the foresters and others are not yet oriented to the ways of incorporating women in forest management. They do not fully appreciate both the complexity and potential of involving women in forestry projects. They need to be sensitised to a perspective on the link between women and nature.

The Perspective

My argument is that to create an effective cadre of women managers of forests, it is not enough to recognise their forestry-related activities. Like in many development projects, women in forestry too can be easily used as cheap and subservient labour. They may be made to work harder than the men to 'prove' themselves. Only token representation may be given to their involvement in the so-called women-related forestry projects. What is generally not addressed is the long-term implication of graduating women into developmental processes—be that forest or water or land management. In a nutshell, our concern here is not of women *per se*, rather it is part of a larger perspective of social equity whereby both women and men are able to manage natural resources to the benefit of their collective empowerment. This is all the more relevant in the light of the economic dependence of poor, rural consumers on forest produce on the one hand and world deforestation touching alarming levels on the other. We have to work out why, where and how to meaningfully link women's needs and activities with the natural regeneration of degraded forests. For this purpose we need to critically examine the pairing of women with nature and the relevance of culture in this paradigm.

The Traditional View of Woman and Nature

In early feminist literature from the West, women and nature were understood to be linked in terms of both being more or less identical with each other. It was assumed that reason, knowledge and virtue were male and/or human attributes and therefore men were held as superior to women and other living beings. The stereotypes about women showed a conspicuous absence of these attributes. Women were compared with nature and found to be passive, emotional and therefore unreasonable. As a result of this perception they tried to reach out and 'prove' themselves by achieving man-like qualities. In his simple manner Gandhi challenged the feminist view by providing another level of discourse. He pointed out that it is not relevant to know if a woman can equally carry a gun and shoot like a man. It is certainly more important to pause and think if shooting is at all good or, beneficial to anyone.

To raise such questions is human and *reflective*. In addition, generally accepted view of opposition between nature and culture also is a part of an outmoded reasoning. Creativity lies in dissolving the opposition between nature and culture by continuous refinement of the natural. Vegetal growth and human growth are part of a single congruence of environmental elements. As traditional gatherers of forest produce for subsistence, women living in and around forests are well aware of deforestation and an urgent necessity of regenerating forests thereby developing a culture of an eco-friendly style of life. Like Ram Chandra Gandhi's (1992:68) Ananya (a tribal woman), one may ask,"How many invasions of modernity can forests suffer without ceasing to be sanctuaries of life, aboriginality and spiritual realisation?" *What then is the contemporary discourse in relation to the steady depletion of non-renewable resources and corresponding excesses of consumption?*

Today, the dominant culture is being equated with what is both masculine and wild. At the same time, the existing norms of masculine (and therefore taken to be human) character of domination are being questioned. The pairing of women with nature is also critically examined in view of the fact that nature itself is considered, in the present politico-economic context, a political construct. In this sense, both gender-based structures and the subjugation of the natural environment are seen as outstanding forms of oppression, providing a basis to diverse forms of domination. Domination of nature and women is hardly any different from other forms of human domination and therefore one needs to make a critique of current systems of domination. This is why one has to continue to review the debate about woman, nature and culture.

Human beings in general and men in particular have come to enjoy rights to dominate/destroy other life forms in the environment and hence we face a host of environmental problems and crises, threatening the very survival of the human race. At this critical juncture in history it appears that the days of celebration of man's control and total subjugation of nature are over. We can begin by outlining the obligations of industry toward the environment and the rural poor women/men.

It is not enough to challenge men's right to control the natural environment. In addition, efforts have to be made to alter the prevailing socio-economic and political institutions. A shift has to be made from subjugation of nature to co-existence with other life forms within the environment. This will obviously negate the 'technique' ideology and its claims to being objective and value-neutral. Instead of rational objectivity and value-neutrality, there has to be placed a positive value on human beings' harmonious co-existence with other life forms in the biosphere. Creating a conscious bias towards the rights of other living creatures is perhaps the only alternative available to promote genetic diversity and to arrest the process of gradual annihilation of the species known to be in existence in the recent past.

It is not the first time in history that prevailing trends of disintegration of human values and the destruction of the environment are being questioned. In ancient India, Buddhism and Jainism derided the social custom of animal sacrifice and advocated the ethical-practices of giving protection to plants and animals. The ideal of non-violence preached by the two religions continues to influence innovative strategies of protest against unjust systems of domination (note the influence of his mother's practices of non-violence on Mahatma Gandhi and his formulation of the Satyagraha movement against the British rule in India). Obverse to protest against unjust systems of domination is the philosophy of harmonious co-existence with other life forms. By and large, even now tribal/rural women harvest plant and animal resources in a moderate and 'wise' manner. Given the opportunity, they can creatively shape the environment friendly utilisation of biological resources.

Such popular environmental movements as the Chipko Andolan (Jain 1984 a and b) and women's movements (see Plumwood 1992a) have conceived women's creative and reflective position vis-a-vis nature. Plumwood (1992b:13) describes this position in contrast to the 'destructive and dualising form of culture'. I would not maintain the idea of contrast. Rather, I would speak of a creative and reflective relationship with nature and its extension or continuation into the domain of culture [cf. Marglin's (1990:114) reference to Zimmermann and Daniel. Both note the absence of a nature-culture dichotomy in non-modern India].

As an answer to disintegrative and divisive systems of politico-economic domination, ecofeminists have forwarded theories of the reconstruction of human society. Ecofeminists insist on an ethic of ecojustice which poses a direct challenge to the very basis of systems of domination. The ethic of ecojustice requires that women form an active (read creative) and reflective relationship with nature whereby they would oppose the disintegrative and divisive forms of the contemporary culture of domination and create a new culture based on the concept of social equity and a harmonious relationship with nature. A harmonious relationship between the natural environment and human beings is also the main aim of environmental movements all over the world. This is, in brief, the creative and reflective nature of the relationship between women and the natural environment. It encompasses also the concept of culture and hence a need to study women's material culture in relation to environmental degradation.

Women and Environmental Degradation

While environmental degradation and shortage of forest products adversely affect all living beings, their impact on women's lives is particularly destructive. Women's responses to results of environmental degradation take place in the context of their social and cultural reality. Causes and effects of and women's responses to environmental degradation are to be understood and explained in terms of social and cultural meaning of gender and class/caste/race-based division of labour and distribution of property and power (Agarwal, 1992:126). Women are victims of environmental degradation and as such they respond to it in the context of their material reality (Agarwal, 1992:123). Most of Agarwal's (1986, 1985, 1984) research focuses on this theme. She has examined the class and gender implications of rural India's environmental degradation.

Let us now discuss our approach to the integration of women into forestry development and then get back to the link between the women and nature-culture continuum.

Approach to Women's Integration into Forestry Development

To the extent women are active and involved members of communities living in and around the forests, their present and potential participation in the management of forests is a viable proposition. In theory, their active participation is to be an integral part of India's new forest policy. The new policy refers to Joint Forest Management (JFM) which was introduced through the 1st June, 1990 Resolution of the Government of India. For implementing this policy, forest departments of the various State governments, non-governmental organisations (NGOs) and researchers have begun networking to define and concretise their courses of action. So far eleven States in India have accepted the concept of JFM for their future programmes of forestry development.

The Concept of JFM

The 1st June, 1990 Resolution of the Government of India represents a marked change in Indian forest policy. The need for change received impetus from the recognition of

i) alarming speed and level of degradation of forests in India
ii) failure of earlier forest policies to regenerate degraded forests
iii) economic dependence of poor, rural consumers (as epitomised in the folk tale 'Chelvi' - a Kannada movie directed by Girish Karnad) on forest products
iv) unplanned exploitation of forest resources for industrial needs
v) exclusion of communities living in and around the forests, from forest management and
vi) growth of continued conflict of interests between the foresters and the poor rural consumers of forest produce and hence a chain of unhealthy relationship of mistrust and suspicion towards each other.

At the policy level, the government has tried to introduce a new approach to forest management and it has decided to strive for making forest dependent people responsible for nurturing and protecting the forests. In return, the new policy accepts the people's right over forest produce. Sharing between the communities (forest protection committees or FPCs) and the forest departments or FDs has to be fair and equitable. In other words, people get the right to enjoy benefits from the forests if they undertake to grow and protect them.

This pattern of managing the forests is given the name of joint forest management (JFM). It implies that both the FDs and the communities living in and around the forests will manage forestry and likewise both will share benefits from the results of their efforts. The role of non-government organisations is that of facilitating the operationalisation of the policy of JFM. Many government resolutions (GRs) passed by the State governments recognise the NGOs as one of the partners in JFM, without according them any benefits of forest products. In terms of benefit-sharing, the partners in JFM are only the FPCs and FDs. All the same the role of NGOs is quite significant in preparing the people to plant and protect trees. They have to undo what the earlier forest policies of the government have done. Alienation from access to and control and management of forests has to stop and the people living in and around forests have to once again, like in the past, become aware of their close links with nature.

Implementation of the New Policy

To implement the new policy of JFM, both the State FDs and NGOs have identified the pressing need for generating communication tools which may help in mutually sharing the available knowledge and experiences of people, NGOs and FDs. In a deliberate manner, FDs, NGOs and researchers have come together to operationalise the concept of JFM. As a result of one such effort (see SPWD Report, 1993), they have come out with the identification of their common needs, which are listed below:

- i) Preparation of communication packages for reducing the credibility gap between foresters and people.
- ii) Preparation of technical packages for
  - (a) training participants in JFM, thereby making all participants take part in micro-planning
  - (b) integrating JFM with other development projects at the village-level
  - (c) creating systems of marketing and allocating benefits of forest management.
- iii) Training programmes to enable mobility of all participants in JFM to higher levels of forest management positions.
- iv) Training programmes to enable people to participate in the industrial management of forest products.
- v) Documentation of existing forest laws, land tenurial systems, ceiling laws etc. for a relatively less cumbersome resolution to conflicts arising out of different ownerships of

lands with trees.

vi) Documentation of women's dependence on forest lands which provide them with fuelwood and non-timber forest products (NTFPs).

vii) Preparation of communicatio‹ packages to sensitise participants in JFM, particularly the foresters about women's needs and roles in forest management.

viii) Documentation of (a) women's experiences of being victimised by environmental degradation and shortage of forest products and (b) women's responses to environmental degradation and management of problems arising out of the shortage of forest products.

Of the above, the multi-media package proposed here is to focus on nos. i, vii, and viii. In this context, we now turn to women in relation to forest management.

Gender Issues in JFM

It is well known that women belonging to communities living in and around the forests are dependent on forest lands and they have specific needs and roles in forest management, though these are hardly recognised as such by the FDs and others concerned with forestry. The NGOs and researchers have documented in their reports and publications the women's forestry-related needs and activities. There is no doubt that in operationalising the concept of JFM, specific needs and roles of women and their rights in the sharing of benefits have to be specially understood and in turn explained to all concerned, so that women do not remain victims of their 'invisible' existence. It is important that this is done at the academic level too, because some among the so-called intelligentsia find the very notion of putting women and forest management together as contradictory. If a multi-media package as proposed here is to be developed at an institution of open learning, which uses the distance education mode, it is essential that the policy-makers as well as colleagues in institutions of open learning be first made aware of new directions in our learning system. They need to encourage study programmes in areas related to women. Research studies dealing with women's activities in forest-related areas have, on the other hand, shown that even when actively engaged in forestry women do not get the benefits of their labour and are often disadvantaged because quite often more powerful participants (read men) in development programmes manage to reap the benefits. Venkateswaran (1993: 2-11) has shown that evaluations of the regeneration of wastelands and the various social forestry programmes by the Institute for Resource Management and Economic Development (1990) and SIDA (1987), respectively, found an overwhelming dominance of males in raising nurseries and completely bypassing women in decision-making. Women are reported to be not even aware of the existence of village forest committees and their functions.

Venkateswaran (1993:6) reports that "a study on the Tamil Nadu social forestry project, for example, pointed out that across four divisions in the state, only six per cent of the total social forestry workers were women". A study (SIDA, 1989) on the Lady Village Forest Workers (LVFWs) and Female Social Forestry Supervisors (FSFSs) in Orissa (quoted in Venkateswaran, 1993:7) found that out of four FSFSs, only one was in the field and the others were given office jobs. Similarly one of the LVFWs was appointed as a typist while those in the field were given section charge with rigid physical targets. They were kept out of extension work. Regarding employment generation, Olsson (1988, mentioned in Venkateswaran 1993: 9) found that 'out of the total work days generated in 1985-86, 70 per cent were given to men and only 30 per cent to women, despite the project mandate that at least 50 per cent of the work opportunities generated would be given to women'. Evaluations of farm forestry (Jain, 1988 and Chambers et al., 1989) have shown that orientation towards cash income from wood has sidelined the supply of minor forest products and hence eliminated the gains of forestry to women. Further, even where farm and community forestry has benefited the community, women have almost no access to and control over the gains received.

Instead of separating or isolating and thereby dumping in a corner and forgetting all about them—as is often done in the name of including women in development programmes, the following reasons can be given for focusing on women's needs and activities in planning JFM programmes.

i) Insofar as the local cultural values inhibit women from expressing themselves in mixed gatherings, they may benefit from special efforts to raise their consciousness about their own needs, capacities, rights and responsibilities.
ii) Owing to the traditional gender discrimination, girls and women lack skills and require further training to improve whatever little skills they may be equipped with.
iii) Because of male migration in many areas, often women have to be *de facto* heads of households but do not find the means of and social approval for upgrading their economic status.
iv) In the prevailing gender based division of labour, women tend to specialise in certain tasks such as the collection of fuelwood, fodder and leaf compost and taking animals to graze. It is necessary to aim at increasing women's productivity and efficiency in these areas so that they get better returns for their labour. (This is not to say that they should not be exposed to other non-traditional tasks so far not associated with them.)
v) Often women do the actual work and men as household heads receive the returns of that labour. It is necessary therefore to recognise at official and legal levels the women's membership of forest protection committees (FPCs) and their freedom to market goods made from raw forest produce.
vi) Whenever women enter the public domain, which is traditionally dominated by men, there are situations of conflict or competition between the women and the men. Before women are sufficiently empowered, they may need, to begin with, their own marketing mechanism for selling

their manufactured goods.

vii) Because of stereotyped roles of women as housewives they are not able to participate in the decision-making processes. Even in projects where they are expected to take on responsibilities of carrying out action plans, they have to follow decisions taken by men. Women are hardly part of the decision-making processes. Explicit mechanisms are required to include women right from the planning and policy making stages of a project.

Women's Cells in Forest Departments

All these reasons appear to be sufficient for planning the JFM activities designed specifically for women. On the other hand, it may be argued that women-specific programmes tend to be largely ignored by the mainstream development planners. Thereafter these remain confined to vested interests via self-serving groups of women and men. For these reasons, the approach of establishing the so-called women's cell in the forest departments (FDs) is not so useful for women's integration into forestry development. As mentioned before, the ethic of ecojustice requires that women build upon the patterns of interaction with forests already existing among them and then form an active (read creative) and reflective relationship with the natural environment. Is there an alternative to the women's cell approach ? We shall go back to our discussion of the link between the women and nature-culture continuum.

Alternative to Women's Cell

While rejecting the approach of setting up women's cells, one cannot help questioning the existing ideas about gender and the distribution of responsibility and benefits between the genders. The prevailing pattern of access to and control and management of natural resources by a few has to be challenged in order to establisning new relationships between people (read both women and men) and the natural environment. More than the dualism of nature and culture, we need to question the ethic of 'pushing' women into wasteland development without increasing their access to and control over and ownership of resources and means of production. Societies torn apart by civil wars, political unrest, ethnic conflicts and socio-economic divisions create disintegrative and divisive forces of domination. These are not easy to overcome. Women in their unfamiliarity with the world of power-games come out with relatively straight (less complex) and non-violent ways of forging links with the natural environment (e.g. Chipko Andolan) and the same is transformed into cultural patterns of women's movements. Often they do challenge the assumptions of current patterns of domination over both women and nature. Here, we need to study both the failure of development strategies for removing such blocks as poverty, deprivation, unemployment and women's placing in terms of the gains of development.

Our understanding of women's material reality (Agarwal, 1992:123) can help us to critically evaluate contemporary society and its disintegrative and divisive systems of politico-economic domination. Ecologists and ecofeminists are together in issuing warnings regarding the disintegration of both the natural environment and human values. It is at this level of discourse we have to contextualise women's integration into the JFM plan of action. The ethic of ecojustice questions the prevailing systems of domination (Jain 1984). Similarly, ecologists challenge the current notions about the link between people and nature and they speak of changing the prevailing patterns of the subjugation of natural resources by a few.

By combining the strategies of both the women's movement and the environmental movement (because both aim at the creation of egalitarian systems), in terms of action, an educational package can be planned for those involved in JFM, including the field staff of FDs and members of FPCs. This initiative from an educational institution would go a long way in implementing the new forest policy. To my mind, institutions of open learning need to take this initiative of expanding the frontiers of knowledge, specially its relation to a new world order. Environmental Studies are certainly going to be in the forefront of future programmes of study in both conventional and open universities.

A Communication Tool in Distance Education Mode

The proposed multi-media package, to be prepared in the distance education mode, would be mainly a communication tool to sensitise the participants in JFM. A similar project is already in existence. It is a communication package on Women in Wasteland Development, prepared by C.P.R. Environmental Education Centre (CPREEC) at Madras. The project has received a positive response from the village women in all the eight districts of Tamil Nadu where this programme has been introduced for the benefit of NGOs. The target group of our proposed educational package includes, as mentioned earlier, the Foresters, NGO functionaries, School Teachers, Health Workers, employed and living in the areas adjacent to forests. All the same, it is proposed to seek collaboration with the CPREEC, Madras, for developing communication techniques. In October 1992, the Communication Research Institute of Australia organised a symposium on information design and its results have been published in a book entitled, *Designing Information for People*, which should be useful for a multi-media presentation of awareness generating information.

Material on women's access to, control and management of the forests and their experiences of being victimised as a result of environmental degradation will form the first component of the package. Based on already available material, it is possible to develop a set of visuals in the form of posters, pamphlets, banners and video films. The second component of the communication package will deal with women's responses to environmental degradation. For this it should be possible to collect the material from already available video films, produced by various agencies. Both components will be mainly for sensitising the foresters and others involved in JFM. In the third or the last part of the package will be case studies to show what has so far been achieved by women in the management of forests. This will be for all those who feel skeptical about women's capacities to nurture and protect the forests. Cases of Sukhomajri, Dasholi Gram Swarajya Mandal, VIKSAT, Bankura, Harda, need to be recorded for both their successes and failures so that participants in JFM can learn from others' experiences.

A core group of experts representing the FDs, NGOs and reseachers will suggest further inputs in the structure of the proposed educational package. They can identify their needs of training in region-specific technologies of afforestation, required for particular ecological zones. The FDs and the Open University may collaborate in preparing technical modules on making the choice of natural regeneration and plantations, and community management of silvicultural operations for the dissemination through distance education to participants in JFM. Similarly, the NGOs can also give their suggestions about such inputs as dovetailing JFM with other rural development projects and improving processing and marketing support systems dealing with non-timber forest products (NTFPs). To present the results of research studies (e.g. Menon 1993; Singh and Vallabh, 1991; Olsson, 1988) collaboration can be planned with researchers in the field of sustainable yield levels, regeneration rates, species productivity, seasonality and changing diversity of both silvicultural systems and natural regeneration processes in degraded forest ecosystems. Studies dealing with fuelwood headloading, sustainable yields and methods for leaf, fodder grass and mulch collection and optimising the availability of quality NTFP to rural consumers can be collected and presented in distance education modules to participants in JFM programmes. This will generate sharing of information on the national scale and enable rural consumers to form both a creative and reflective relationship with the natural environment.

Besides sharing information, technical inputs can be provided on nursery techniques, wasteland development techniques, water and land management, coir weaving for ropes and mats, palm leaf basketry, grafting and layering etc. Another package, in the future, can provide a legal manual about tenurial issues. The NGOs working with communities living in and around forest areas have time and again had to resolve conflicts arising out of a *de facto* management system without a *de jure* status. Often settlement and nistar rights are not clear about the definition of user-groups. With the introduction of JFM and its operational units, the FPCs, their legal status and tenure security will have to be made clear to participants in the JFM programme. The NGOs have faced the problems but can do precious little about the prevailing confusion in this regard. It will be useful for them to have handbooks dealing with separate land tenurial laws. This will be a major input in the proposed educational package. MARG, Delhi, has already brought out a publication entitled *The Land Acquisition Act and You.* The Centre for Environmental Law in Delhi has expertise available in this field.

Conclusion

Management of the vital resource of forests can be ensured by applying appropriate techniques of forestry management, protection and maintenance of existing forests with the active participation of the people, specially women. They have been keeping the capital intact and yet providing for basic needs of fuel, fodder and other non-timber forest products. Regeneration of degraded forest lands and efforts to increase their productivity are dependent on the degree of people's participation in forestry. People specially women will participate in forestry insofar they have an interest in using forest products. For example, based on a successful pilot project at Arabari in W. Bengal in 1972, about 1250 village forest protection committees (with women members) decided to protect an area of one and a half lakh hectares of degraded forests in West Bengal. This gave an impetus to the central government to adopt the policy of joint forest management. Schemes for developing degraded forest lands are also likely to boost generation of employment opportunities in tribal/rural areas. Further, the socio-economic crisis arising out of the shortage of fuelwood and fodder can be handled by making tree-management a concern of rural/tribal consumers, of women headloaders. A communication package, comprising mainly audio/video inputs, posters, pamphlets etc., supported by media notes and other print-material can cover the above analysis of the present situation in a format which can be taken to the people, to the policy makers and policy implementers in a direct and effective manner. This will in turn build bridges between the present owners of forests (the FDs) and the people. Only cooperation between the two and their commitment can save India's forest resources.

Should the question of saving India's forests be or not be a concern of an open learning centre ? Should we continue to teach subjects already covered by conventional universities ? Should we at an open university broaden our vision to include the preparation of such educational packages as proposed in this chapter? These are the questions before us and we need to answer them without delay.

REFERENCES

Agarwal, Bina, (1984). "Rural Women and the High Yielding Variety Rice Technology". *Economic and Political Weekly,* 10(13, 31).

_____, (1985). "Work Participation of Rural Women in the Third World : Some Data and Conceptual Biases". *Economic and Political Weekly,* 20(51, 52).

_____, (1986). *Cold Hearths and Barren Slopes : The Woodfuel Crises in the Third World.* Delhi: Allied Publishers.

_____, (1992). "The Gender and Environment Debate : Lessons from India". *Feminist Studies,* 18(1):119-158.

Gandhi, Ram Chandra, (1992). *Sita's Kitchen: A Testimony of Faith and Inquiry.* New Delhi: Penguin Books.

Jain, S. (1984a). "Women and People's Ecological Movement : A Case Study of Women's Role in the Chipko Movement in Uttar Pradesh". *Economic and Political Weekly*, 13: 1788-1794.

Jain, S. (1984b). "Standing Up for Trees". *UNASYLVA,* 36(4) : 12-20.

Jain, S. (1988). *Case Studies of Farm Forestry and Wasteland Development in Gujarat, India.* (Community Forestry Case Studies Series no 1), FAO (UN).

Marglin, F.A. (1990), "Smallpox in Two System of Knowledge". In F.A. Marglin and S.A. Marglin (eds) *Dominating Knowledge.* Oxford: Clarendon Press. pp. 102-144.

Menon, G. (1993). "A Brief Exposition of Ecology-related Changes in Tribal Women's Work and Status". Unpublished Paper presented at a *Workshop on Gender and the Rural Environment* at the Institute of Rural Management, Anand, April 1993.

Olsson, Gunilla (1988). *Employment and Income Generation in Social Forestry: A Case Study from Orissa.* ILO: Geneva

Plumwood, Val (1992a). *Gender and Ecology and the Mastery of Nature.* London: Routledge.

Plumwood, Val (1992b). "Feminism and Ecofeminism: Beyond the Dualistic Assumption of Women, Men and Nature". *The Ecologist,* 22(1): 8-13.

Singh, K. and Vallabh, V. (1991). "People's Participation in Forest Management: Experience of Van Panchayats in U.P. Hills". *Wasteland News,* October 1991.

SPWD, (1993). *Joint Forest Management : Concept and Opportunities.* (Proceedings of the National Workshop in August 1992) New Delhi: Society for Promotion of Wastelands Development.

Venkateswaran, S. (1993). Government Approaches to Natural Research Management: Women's Participation and Impact on Women. Unpublished paper presented at a *Workshop on Gender and the Rural Environment* at the Institute of Rural Management, Anand, April 1993.

LIBRARY AND INFORMATION SCIENCE COURSES FOR WOMEN

NEELA JAGANNATHAN and UMA KANJILAL

Introduction

The progress made in the field of Library and Information Science (LIS) in the past three decades indicates that LIS cannot be merely categorized as belonging to the Social Science group. It has systematically and scientifically developed into an independent interdisciplinary field. The tremendous progress made in LIS has posed a challenge for both:

* the LIS teachers teaching at different levels i.e., from certificate in LIS to master's degree in LIS; and
* the librarians working in different type of libraries such as, National, Public, Academic, and other Special Libraries in the country.

In India there are about 140 universities providing LIS courses at various levels. Realizing that traditional universities are unable to meet the growing demand for trained LIS professionals in the country, B.R. Ambedkar Open University, Hyderabad was the first Open University in the country to start the Bachelor's degree programme in Library and Information Science in 1985 through the distance mode for in-service professionals. The response to this programme was tremendous. However, the only limitation was that it was meant for the library professionals residing in the state of Andhra Pradesh. In order to fulfil the rising demand for LIS courses in India the Indira Gandhi National Open University (IGNOU), New Delhi launched the Bachelor's degree programme (BLIS) in 1989. The BLIS programme of IGNOU has been quite successful and has been able to cater to the growing demand for LIS professionals in the country. Imbued by the success of the BLIS programme and also inspired by the requests and demands from the previous BLIS students as well as the other in-service personnel, the University decided to launch the Master's degree programme in LIS (MLIS) from 1994. Interestingly, it has been noticed that a large number of women candidates are taking admission to the BLIS programme. The ratio of women candidates is 42.7% for the present batch (1993-94). The various problems of the women students undertaking the BLIS programme and the suggested strategies for facilitating their study are dealt with in this paper.

LIS Courses: Indian Scenario

The history of Library and Information Science education in India is hardly sixty years old. Initially it used to be either on-job training or part-time courses conducted by various professional associations. Gradually, the full time Library Science programmes at various levels such as Bachelor's degree, Master's degree, M.Phil, and Ph.D. programmes were started by the traditional universities in the country.

Table 1 indicates the various levels of LIS courses in the conventional institutions in the country.

TABLE 1

NUMBER OF LIS COURSES AT DIFFERENT LEVELS IN CONVENTIONAL UNIVERSITIES

S. No.	Level of courses	No. of Instt.
1.	Higher secondary (10+2)	1
2.	Certificate in LIS	87
3.	Diploma in LIS	18
4.	Bachelor's degree in LIS	91
5.	Bachelor of Arts in LIS(3 yr duration)	02
6.	Master's degree in LIS	57
7.	M.Phil in LIS	05
8.	Ph.D in LIS	39
9.	Associateship in LIS	02

Apart from these LIS is also imparted through various correspondence institutions and Open Universities in India (Table 2).

TABLE 2

LIS COURSES THROUGH DISTANCE MODE

S.No.	University	CLIS	DLIS	BLIS	MLIS
I	**Correspondence Institutions:-**				
1.	Annamalai University			✔	✔
2.	Awadhesh Pratap Singh University, Rewa			✔	
3.	Kakatiya University, Warangal			✔	
4.	University of Kashmir	✔			
5.	Kurukshetra University				✔
6.	University of Madras	✔		✔	✔
7.	Madurai Kamraj University	✔		✔	
8.	Punjabi University, Patiala		✔		
9.	Shri Venkateshwara Univ., Tirupati	✔			
II	**Open Universities:-**				
1.	B. R. Ambedkar Open University, Hyderabad			✔	✔*
2.	IGNOU, New Delhi			✔	✔
3.	Kota Open University		✔		✔*
4.	Nalanda Open University			✔*#	
5.	Yashwantrao Chavan Maharashtra Open University			✔*	

* Under preparation

PG Diploma equivalent to BLS

BLIS and MLIS Programmes of IGNOU

The Bachelor's degree programme in Library and Information Science (BLIS) of IGNOU was launched in 1989. After successfully conducting the BLIS programme for the past five years, the University launched the Master's degree programme in Library and Information Science (MLIS) from 1994. While the objective of the BLIS programme is to impart basic skills and training required to manage and organize different types of libraries, the MLIS programme is meant for development and training of high level skills required for manning higher positions in libraries and information centres in the country. The main aim of these two programmes is professional development and betterment of employment opportunities for those who are already employed in libraries and information centres.

The currriculum for both these programmes are innovative and many new features have been added. Two new courses e.g., Information Services and Computer Basics and Applications have been added to the curriculum of BLIS. A practical exposure to the computer and handling of library software package CDS/ISIS has been incorporated as a part of the course in Computer Basics and Application. Keeping in mind the fact that the present society is gradually evolving as an Information Society, the curriculum for the MLIS programme has been designed in such a way that the LIS professionals are trained to meet the requirements of the society. The core courses of the MLIS programme are devoted to various aspects of information handling, management and application of information technology, and there are electives designed to meet the requirements of specialized skills like preservation of library materials, research methodology, technical writing etc. The curriculum also incorporates practical training in the handling of modern information technologies such as CD-ROM, online searching of databases, database design and searching with the help of library software like LIBSYS and CDS/ISIS.

IGNOU has incorporated a number of innovative features in the BLIS and MLIS programmes viz.,

* flexible entry regulation
* self-pacing without any time-place barrier
* providing students support services including counselling sessions and library facilities
* imparting high quality education through multi-media packages
* use of computers and modern sophisticated communication technologies like radio, television and teleconferencing.

Thus, IGNOU's LIS programmes have become very popular and have set a new trend of education through distance mode in India.

Profile of Women Students for LIS Courses of IGNOU

The fact that LIS is a women intensive profession can be well judged from Table 3 (Coursewise Gender Profile of Admissions of Students in 1994).

TABLE 3

COURSEWISE GENDER PROFILE OF ADMISSIONS OF STUDENTS IN 1994

S. No.	Course	Male		Female		Total
		Number	%	Number	%	
1.	BPP	7351	75.23	2421	24.77	9772
2.	BDP	18625	74.18	6484	25.82	25109
3.	BLIS	733	57.27	547	42.73	1280
4.	MP	17227	93.10	1277	6.90	18504
5.	ACC	28	10.45	240	89.55	268
6.	ANC	22	36.67	38	63.33	60
7.	CFN	425	12.59	2951	87.41	3376
8.	CIG	255	31.84	546	68.16	801
9.	DCE	283	58.47	201	41.53	484
10.	DCH	103	62.42	62	37.58	165
11.	DCO	925	84.17	174	15.83	1099
12.	DIM	1175	97.27	33	2.73	1208
13.	DNHE	585	47.68	642	52.32	1227
14.	DRD	1166	67.28	567	32.72	1733
15.	MADE	43	87.76	6	12.24	49
16.	PGDDE	283	63.30	162	36.40	445
17.	PGDHE	222	56.06	174	43.94	396
18.	PGDHFM	2696	90.47	284	9.53	2980
19.	PGDHRM	1880	80.72	449	19.28	2329
20.	PGDMM	4761	94.26	290	5.74	5051
21.	PGDOM	2233	94.74	124	5.26	2357
		61,021	77.54	17,672	22.46	78693

It is clear from Table 3 that the overall percentage of male and female learners are 77.54% and 22.46% respectively. It is also noticed while perusing statistics that apart from the stereotyped continuing education courses of feminine interest viz., Application Course in Child Care (ACC), Application Course in Nutrition (ANC), Certificate in Food and Nutrition (CFN), Certificate in Guidance (CIG), Diploma in National Health Education (DNHE), in which the percentage of women admitted ranges from 50% to 90%, there are only three other professional courses that have a high percentage of women candidates. These are:

* Post-Graduate Diploma in Higher Education (PGDHE) - 43.94%
* Bachelor of Library and Information Science (BLIS) - 42.73%
* Diploma in Creative Writing in English (DCE) - 41.53%

TABLE 4

GENDER PROFILE OF BLIS STUDENTS

Year	Male		Female		Total
	Number	%	Number	%	
1989-90	817	63.4	471	36.6	1288
1990-91	1345	71.81	527	28.2	1872
1991-92	837	57.3	624	42.7	1461
1992-93	814	55.3	659	44.7	1473
1993-94	733	57.3	547	42.7	1280

While analyzing the student enrolment trends for BLIS for the past five years (Table 4) indicate that the percentage of women candidates is steadily increasing. It has increased from 36.67% in 1989-90 to 42.77% in 1993-94. The gender profile is shown in Figure 1. Though the BLIS Programme is only meant for those who are already employed in the profession, the percentage of women candidates taking up the course is quite impressive. This reflects the fact that women are not merely taking it up to accumulate degrees, but are already employed and have taken it up for career advancement. The first batch of BLIS students were awarded degrees in

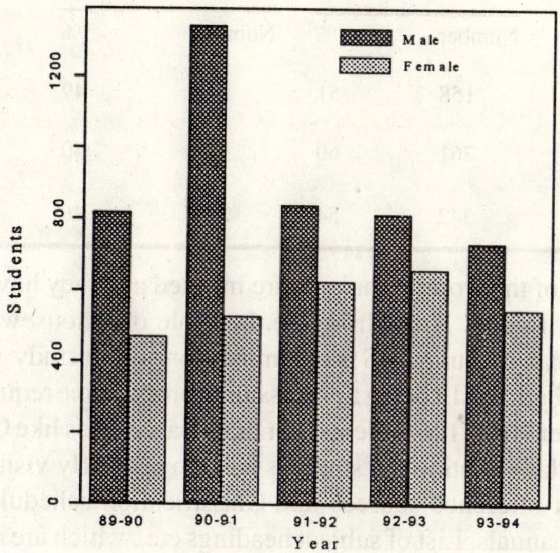

Fig. 1: Bar Chart of Gender Profile of BLIS Students

1992 at the third convocation. On examining the list of students who have successfully completed their studies and were awarded BLIS degree in the third, fourth and fifth convocations, held in 1992, 1993 and 1994 respectively (Table 5), it is clear that the percentage of successful female students is lesser than the male students. Even though women students have to face many difficulties in pursuing their studies as compared to male students, the pass percentage is quite impressive. IGNOU started giving gold medals to first rank holders in different disciplines from the fifth convocation in 1994. The interesting fact is that two women candidates were awarded gold medals for the BLIS programme.

TABLE 5

GENDER PROFILE OF SUCCESSFUL BLIS STUDENTS

Year	Male		Female		Total
	Number	%	Number	%	
1992	158	51	152	49	310
1993	261	60	178	40	439
1994	342	54	299	46	641

Most of the women students are married and they have to look after their family. Apart from the dual role of a housewife and a professional, pursuing LIS programmes for further study increases strain on them. BLIS being a professional programme requires extra involvement from the students. For practical courses like Cataloguing and Classification the students have to regularly visit libraries to consult reference sources like Classification schedules, Cataloguing manuals, List of subject headings etc., which are not easily accessible. Moreover they have to visit libraries from time to time to do their assignments. Thus visit to study centres is a must. Since the BLIS programme at present has only 34 study centres, the students face difficulty in attending the counselling sessions and utilization of library facilities. They have to travel long distances to reach study centres. This difficulty is further enhanced in the case of women students, for whom it may be absolutely impossible at times to leave home for the purpose. Thus a serious thought needs to be given in this direction to facilitate the women students. The University has so far not given much thought to this matter, and it is time that certain special provisions are made for the BLIS women students so as to make the programme fruitful.

Strategies for LIS Women Students

A recent survey conducted by Neela Jagannathan (1993) indicates that i) there are requests for separate study centres for women students and ii) the working hours of the study centres and their libraries should be convenient to female students. Housewives want the study centres to be open on all working days between 10 a.m. to 4 p.m. so that they can study during the day time after their husbands and children leave for work and school respectively.

The BLIS women students are mostly employed, therefore the problems faced by them are of a more complex nature. The evening timings do not suit them since they have to perform household duties after coming back from work. They also have restrictions for travelling alone at night. Again, on holidays it is difficult for them to visit the study centres as husband and children are at home and they expect their wives/mothers to spend more time with them. Hence, it is imperative to provide special facilities for women students.

The strategies that would benefit the students in general are:

* Issuing of books to facilitate the students to work at home.
* Special arrangements should be made with local public and academic libraries for provision of reference books frequently needed for assignments. This will ensure easy access to the students and they can frequently visit libraries for consulting reference sources.
* More attention should be paid to the multi-media aspects of imparting education through the distance mode. Production of good quality audio/video programmes can solve the problems faced by distant students to a great extent. Issuing of A/V cassettes will enable the students to study effectively at home.
* Emphasis should be given to broadcast A/V programmes through radio and television. This will ensure equitable distribution of course specific programmes to a larger population of students spread far and wide.

Though the strategies suggested above are meant for the students in general, their implementation can solve the problems faced by the BLIS women students to a great extent. At present IGNOU telecasts its video programmes on the Doordarshan Channel at 6.30 a.m. on Monday, Wednesday and Friday. This timing does not suit the women students as they have to get their children ready for school and make preparation to go to office for themselves as well as for their husbands. Therefore it is necessary to change the timings of the programmes so that the women can also watch them. Thus a serious thought needs to be given to all the factors that can facilitate women in pursuing their studies effectively.

Conclusion

The percentage of women students taking up BLIS programme has risen from 36.6% in 1989-90 to 42.7% in 1993-94. In 1992 the first batch of BLIS students received their degrees, in which out of the total of 310 students 152 were women. In the last convocation (1994) 299 women students received their degrees. Thus the percentage of successful women candidates is also quite impressive. It has been found that women BLIS students have to face many problems to pursue their studies as they have the dual responsibility of their profession and home. Taking into account all the difficulties faced by women it is essential to devise some strategies that can facilitate them to successfully pursue their studies. Well set out facilities specifically meant for women will not only help those who have presently taken up the LIS programmes of IGNOU, it will also inspire many more women to take up the programmes in future.

REFERENCES

Association of Indian Universities and The Commonwealth of Learning (1991). *Directory of Distance Education Institutions*. Part 1: India.New Delhi:AIU. .

IGNOU, New Delhi (1994) BLIS Programme Guide.

IGNOU, New Delhi (1994) MLIS Programme Guide.

Jagannathan, Neela (1993). *Library facilities of IGNOU: A case study*. Dissertation submitted for Master's Degree in Library Science, Bombay University, Bombay.

Vashishth, Shobha (1990). *Bharat mein pustakalay evam suchna vigyan ki shiksha evam prashikshan*. Unpublished dissertation for MLIS degree at Jivaji University, Gwalior.

GENDER EQUALITY IN DISTANCE EDUCATION: AN ANALYSIS OF COURSE MATERIALS OF IGNOU

M.D. USHADEVI

The uneven spread of education among men and women has caught the attention of the concerned all over the world. This has been a matter of even greater concern in the developing nations. The low level of education among women as compared to men has been attributed to several factors. One of them is education *per se* which is found to perpetuate inequality between the two sexes in terms of access, participation and performance. Examining the existing conventional education system, one comes across several criticisms levelled against it. One criticism is on its discriminatory characteristic in terms of its structure, content and practice which inhibits women's participation and performance. In this context feminist critics go out to prove the negative role played by the school system in terms of reproducing the socialization norms that reinforce traditional patriarchal ideologies, the sexual discriminatory practices through its content, teaching practices, teacher behaviour, perceptions etc. All these factors are found to perpetuate inequality between the sexes.

While the educational content mirrors the subservient status of women in society through its textbooks and other learning materials, even teachers themselves are found to perpetuate the discriminating practices through teaching, assessment and other curricular interactions. Such discriminatory tendencies by teachers are attributed to the deficient and inadequate teacher preparatory programmes that one undergoes prior to undertaking a teaching assignment (Mbilinyi,1985).

Even though at the inception of its educational policies in independent India, the Government recognised the need to develop a curriculum which promoted equality between the sexes, and the Education Commission (1964-66) articulated this issue by recommending that Indian text books should not promote archaic, sexist stereotypes. Further, the constitution of various commissions and committees in the country to look into the issues of women's education are testimony to the concerns exhibited by the National and State governments. Of these the Status Survey Towards Equality (1974) and the National Perspective Plan for Women (1988) are noteworthy. The recent New Educational Policy (1986) has also not lagged behind in declaring its commitment to removing educational disparities between men and women. It reflects deeper concerns for women's education by devoting a separate section on Education for Women's Equality which outlines several fresh approaches to tackling the issue of women's education.

It is with the basic objective of promoting equality and social justice that several alternatives have been provided at various stages of education. Part-time and continuing education, correspondence education and open universities have been specifically launched to cater to the demands of those sections of the population including women who for various reasons cannot utilise the opportunities provided by the conventional educational system. The rigidities imposed by the conventional systems in terms of attendance and other entry requirements pose hazards to these sections of the population. It is in this context that the Programme of Action (1986) declares that the open university system in a country like ours would augment opportunities for higher education and ensure access and that it would be cost effective and promote a flexible and innovative system of education.

It is along these lines that Indira Gandhi National Open University was launched with the avowed objective of democratising educational opportunities across regions, genders, castes and classes. As compared to other distance educational programmes, IGNOU's programmes appear to be quite popular and are in great demand owing to its special features like relaxed entry regulations, learner's autonomy in terms of choice of courses, a flexible time-place schedule well-organised student support services through its Regional/Study Centres and the innovative multi-media instructional packages. In fact, the course materials of IGNOU have won accolades from both academics and non-academics owing to their self-instructional features which are developed along the lines of programmed instructional techniques for effective individualised learning. It is no wonder that the IGNOU course materials are sought after even by some conventional universities for their regular courses of study.

Despite the attributive features of IGNOU, there are, however, contain disturbing trends in its performance which is a matter of concern for planners, policy makers and educationists. A preliminary analysis of the enrolment trends and staff composition in IGNOU has revealed that there is a tilt in the enrolment towards urban, male and general sections of population rather than female, rural and SC/ST population for whose chief benefit the open university was started. Even the gender profile of IGNOU staff reveals a male bias in terms of academic, technical and administrative staff both in regular and contractual assignments (Jagannathan, 1991). Anyway it is too early to draw generalisations as the university is still at an early stage.

It is noticed that generally two related problems emerge regarding women's access to and successful participation in distance mode courses: (i) the male construction and ownership of knowledge and (ii) the invisibility of women in course materials (Elizabeth Burge and Helen Lenskyj, 1990). It is these theoretical postulates which have set an agenda for the present research. The present study seeks to find out to what extent women have been represented and are visible in the course materials prepared by IGNOU for distance learners. In essence the study seeks to find out whether an equal amount of importance has been given to women as much as to men while developing and designing course materials.

It is surprising to note that despite glorious declarations by the various commissions and committees to remove the gender bias in the curriculum, discrimination in one form or another has persisted in the curriculum. This may be perhaps due to the fact that there has been no systematic and comprehensive evaluation of the Indian textbooks to analyse the sex role-models to determine as to what extent the declared policy has been effected. Research efforts in this direction have been sporadic and have had limited scope. Further researches dealing with issues of gender discrimination in the course materials of distance education programmes are conspicuous by their absence. Thus, a need has been felt by the researcher to look into the issue of any possible gender discrimination in the course materials of IGNOU. Against this backdrop, the present study is set with the following objectives:

* to examine the extent of representation given to women as compared to men in the preparation and developmental stage
* to examine the extent of visibility of women in the course content.

Methodology

The present study has adopted a case study design with content analysis technique to examine the above objectives. A case study of one of the Post-Graduate Diploma Programmes of IGNOU has been carried out for the purposes of the present study. Content analysis of the course materials belonging to this particular programme has been done. Frequency counts have been used to represent the extent of women's visibility in course materials. The analysis has been quantitative, qualitative, and inferential.

Before presenting the analysis of the data, it would be in place here to present a brief resume of the postgraduate diploma programme selected for the purpose of the present study. The Postgraduate Diploma in Higher Education (PGDHE) is basically developed in response to recommendations of the National Policy on Education (NPE) 1986 with a view to providing necessary knowledge, understanding and skills pertaining to higher education to university and college teachers (IGNOU,1991). The programme is meant for a target audience of those who teach or aspire to teach in universities, colleges and other institutions of higher learning. The programme has the following underlying objectives:

a) to acquire a perspective regarding the system of higher education, its context, its functions and its linkages with other systems;
b) to develop professional competencies that a university teacher ought to have; and
c) to develop readiness to undertake reforms and innovations in the practice of the teaching profession.

The programme consists of five courses, one of them being a project (Course 5). The other four courses are:

Course 1 : Higher Education: Its Context and Linkages
Course 2 : Instruction in Higher Education
Course 3 : Higher Education: The Social-Psychological Field
Course 4 : Planning and Management of Higher Education.

Each of the above courses consists of four blocks (printed booklets of self-instructional material) thematically linked to each other, and a few audio and video cassettes.

The rationale for selecting this particular programme (PGDHE) for the purpose of the present research has emanated from the following:

* The researcher herself was a student of this programme and hence had access to the course materials.
* The programme is specifically meant for college and university teachers, who form an integral part of the educational system and who have a significant role to play in eliminating gender discrimination if any, in the classroom during curricular transactions. It is presumed that the effect of gender bias in a course like this would certainly have a spillover effect on the participants when they start practising teaching.

For the purpose of content analysis, one block from each of the courses is taken. Each block (booklet) in the inside cover pages indicates the composition of the course committee, course contributors, editors and production personnel. An analysis of these cover pages would indicate the extent of women's representation on the course curriculum, preparation and development. Each self-instructional unit in the booklet consists of three sections: the opening section, main body of the texts and the ending of the unit. The opening section consists of the title and number of lessons, outline of unit contents, the objectives and an introduction. The main text/body is the actual content. There are also illustrations/examples/diagrams/flow charts, pictures and cartoons to break the monotony of reading the texts, to make the self-learning interesting and exciting, and thereby to sustain the motivation of the learners. Further, there are also self-check exercises and in-text activities which ensure feedback and greater involvement of the learners.

For the present study the content analysis of the course materials is done both coursewise and blockwise. Before actual content analysis of the course materials is done, an attempt has been made at the outset, to find out the extent of representation given to women as compared to men at the preparatory/developmental stage of the course materials.

Construction and Ownership of Knowledge

For developing course materials, IGNOU has set up an expert committee consisting of eminent people in the field. This committee decides the curriculum and content density for the course concerned. The course developers are supposed to have pedagogical competencies to do the complex job of researching, writing and editing. For writing contents for the course, there are course contributors/writers who either work individually or in a team. Further, these course writers comprise both full-time and part-time staff. While the former are the faculty of IGNOU, the latter are drawn from various conventional colleges and universities. Besides course contributors, there are also editors, coordinators and production personnel, all from IGNOU.

In this analysis, an attempt has been made to find out the extent of involvement of women in the development stage of the course, as revealed in Table 1.

TABLE 1
REPRESENTATION OF WOMEN AND MEN ON THE EXPERT COMMITTEE

Course	Women	Men	Total
Course I	4	23	27
Course II	4	23	27
Course III	4	23	27
Course IV	4	23	27

It could be seen from the table that there is an apparent imbalance in the representation of women on the expert committee as compared to men. There are only four women as against 23 men in all the courses. The same four women are noticed in all the course expert committees. Incidentally three of these four women are Delhi-based, and only one is from Mother Teresa Women's University, Madras. One of the reasons for such an imbalance could be non-availability of women at the topmost academic ladder. As the members for the Expert Committee are normally drawn from the Who's Who of Education and most of these people are in the top echelons of the academic world, women may be a 'rare commodity' therein.

A further analysis of the composition of course contributors/ writers has revealed the following (Table 2):

TABLE 2
REPRESENTATION OF WOMEN AND MEN ON THE PANEL OF COURSE CONTRIBUTORS/WRITERS/ TECHNICIANS/PRODUCTION PERSONNEL

Course	Women	Men	Total
Course I	5	10	15
Course II	4	12	16
Course III	5	11	16
Course IV	3	16	19

Even here it is clear that women are underrepresented as compared to men. These are by and large senior faculty members teaching in conventional universities and colleges. The overall representation of women teachers in the university teaching departments and degree colleges is one-sixth and one-fourth respectively (*India*, 1990). As such women may be poorly represented here. Another plausible reason could be that women teachers were approached for course writing assignments which were perhaps declined due to their prior preoccupations or women teachers were never approached at all for the purpose. In any case the analysis reveals that there is a tilt towards men while selecting course writers. The question, 'Is it because the people who select course writers are by and large men and therefore have tended to select men only?' needs further probing. However, it would augur well for a university which is named after a woman to give at least equal if not more representation to women on its academic and allied bodies.

The Course Content

The content of the course materials of PGDHE of IGNOU is analysed for any possible gender biases. Both the textual and pictorial contents have been examined for the purpose. These materials analysed are as follows:

Unit 1 'The progressive Social role of a University teacher in India' under Course 1—Higher Education: its Context and Linkages.

TABLE 3
LANGUAGE USED BY THE WRITERS WHILE ADDRESSING THE TEACHERS

Unit Components	Course I			Course II			Course III			Course IV		
	M	F	B	M	F	B	M	F	B	M	F	B
Introduction			9	2								
Objectives												
Unit content	2		66	116		2	1		88	14		91
Intext activity				6		1						
Self-check exercises			2	3								
Let us sum up				2								
Examples/ Illustrations	7			17						2		
Unit-end activities			2	1								
Points for Discussion				3								
Total	9		79	150		3	1		88	16		91

M - Male Centred, F - Female Centred, B - Both Male and Female Centred

Unit 2	'Instruction in a Systemic Perspective' under Course 2 - Instruction in Higher Education
Unit 3	'Psychology of Learning and Teaching in Higher Education' under Course 3 - Higher Education: The Social-Psychological field.
Unit 4	'Management of Instruction in Higher Education' under Course 4 - Planning and Management of Higher Education.

All these course materials have one common audience i.e. the university and the college teachers. Hence the teachers are referred to in the content more frequently in one way or another. It is noticed that the content on the whole does not reveal any gender discrimination either in terms of elevating the status/role of men teachers or denigrating the status/role of women teachers. The content in all the courses is free of any gender biases. Hence IGNOU could be credited for promoting the equality of sexes through its course contents.

Language of the Content

An attempt has also been made to analyse the language used in the content to determine gender biases, if any in the textual contents. It may be noticed that the language used at different stages of content presentation has lent itself to gender biases. However, it is at the stage of presentation of unit content and while presenting examples and illustrations that gender biases are found to creep in more frequently. It is noticed that only in Course-II, gender bias is conspicuous to the extent of cent per cent. This is a course which speaks about Instruction in Higher Education in general and Instruction in Systemic Perspective in particular. As said earlier since the course is targeted at teachers in colleges and university teaching departments, it is expected that both men and women teachers should be addressed by the course writers to an equal extent. However, it appears from the pronouns used in the language that the course is addressed to male teachers only. Although, it is he-man language [as Dale Spender (1980) has called it] which is universally used and the formal rules of English grammar prescribe that man in the sense of mankind should be understood as including both men and women, yet empirical evidence indicates that the use of 'he' language is not understood as inclusive of 'she' language in educational situations (Miller and Swift, 1977).

Course-II also reveals male-centred language to a greater extent than the other three blocks while citing examples and illustrations. It may be noted from Table 4, that the language used in the other three courses has given equal emphasis to both genders as course writers seem to be quite cautious while using pronouns (she/he and her/his). Hence to this extent, it could be said that IGNOU does promote gender equality through its course materials.

TABLE 4
REPRESENTATION OF MEN AND WOMEN FIGURES IN THE DIAGRAMS AND CARTOONS

Unit Components	Course I			Course II			Course III			Course IV		
	M	F	B	M	F	B	M	F	B	M	F	B
Pictures/ Illustrations/ Diagrams	-	-	-	5	2	-	-	-	-	-	-	-
Cartoons	7	-	-	1	-	-	-	-	1	13	-	-
Total	7	-	-	6	2	-	-	-	1	13	-	-

M = Males only. F = Females only. B = Both.

The course writers have also interspersed pictorial illustrations/ diagrams, cartoons along with the textual contents to reinforce self-learning as well as for breaking the monotony of drab reading.

For this analysis, only those pictures/cartoons which showed men and/or women figures have been picked up. There were altogether seven such pictures out of 22 cartoons. It may be noticed from the analysis that with the exception of Course-III, in the remaining three courses, only figures representing men were presented to drive home a point. There are the pictures which show a teacher teaching or performing his task and students inside the classroom. In no picture women are shown to be teaching or interacting with students. On the other hand, only men teachers in the classrooms are shown. Even while showing the students, one can see that male students either outnumber female students or they are sitting on the front benches while female students occupy the back benches. Cartoons by the famous cartoonist R.K. Laxman mock at the educational system through the actions of either students or teachers or both. Invariably only male characters are used for the purpose.

Findings and Discussion

The study made an attempt to examine the possible gender biases in the course materials of IGNOU. It was assumed that for promoting equality between sexes, it was necessary that course materials should present gender bias-free contents. However, the existing empirical evidence points out that owing to traditional ownership and construction of knowledge by male-dominated society, gender discrimination still persists in terms of content and language presentation in the distance mode of education. A case study of course units on 'The progressive social role of a university teacher in India'; 'Psychology of learning and teaching in Higher Education'; and 'Management of instruction in Higher Education' of the Post-graduate Diploma in Higher Education was done. As far as construction and ownership of knowledge in these courses are concerned, male domination is obvious as women are found to be poorly represented both on the experts committees and on the panel of course writers. There are only four women out of 27 on the expert committee and 3-5 out of 15-19 in the course contributors' list. Hence there is a need for giving more representation to women teachers to correct imbalances.

The content materials of these courses do not reveal any gender biases. However, the language used in the textual content does display a sexist bias only in one course out of the four courses examined. In the unit named 'Instruction in a systemic perspective', it appears that the course writers have only male teachers in view. In the remaining three courses, the course writers have given equal importance to both men and women. The course writers of these three courses are found to be cautious in addressing both male and female teachers while referring to teachers in Higher Education. So far as pictorial illustrations and cartoons are concerned, there is a definite gender bias.

Thus, the findings of this research imply that whatever sexist-bias is revealed in the language, the textual content and pictures/cartoons, these aspects need to be corrected and a more balanced treatment of men and women needs to be presented to distance learners. The present study is only a small attempt that deals with a limited sample of course materials from only one programme of IGNOU. Hence, the findings may have limitations for broader generalizations. Perhaps, content analyses of course materials on a large scale in a few undergraduate programmes offered by IGNOU may provide a better picture about gender biases in distance education and may have broader implications for a future course of action to promote gender equality.

REFERENCES

Burge Elizabeth and Helen Lenskyj (1990). 'Women Studying in Distance Education: Issues and Principles', *Journal of Distance Education*, Vol. V(i), pp. 20-37.

Dale Spender (1980). *Man-made Language*, London: Routledge.

IGNOU (1991). *Information Brochure*, School of Education.

India 1990/A Reference Manual, New Delhi: Ministry of Information and Broadcasting, Government of India.

Jagannathan, Neela (1991). 'Gender Equality in Education - IGNOU's Role', *University News*, Vol. XXIX (5), pp.1-5.

Mbilinyi, M.J. (1985). "Women in Education" in *The International Encyclopedia of Education*, (eds) Torsten Husen and T.N. Postlethwaite, Oxford: Pergamon Press.

Miller and Swift, K. (1977). *Words and Women*, New York: Anchor Books.

National Perspective Plan for Women: 1988-2000 AD, Department of Women and Child Development. New Delhi: Ministry of Human Resource Development, Government of India.

New Education Policy - 1986, Ministry of Human Resource Development, New Delhi: Government of India.

The Programme of Action - 1986, Ministry of Human Resource Development, New Delhi: Government of India.

The Report of the Education Commission -1964-66, (1966). Ministry of Education and Culture, New Delhi: Government of India.

Towards Equality (1974). The Report of the Committee on the

Status of Women in India, Department of Social Welfare, Ministry of Education and Social Welfare, New Delhi: Government of India.
Works by Liberal Feminists like Stacey Judith (1965), Wolf Margery (1985), Desta Asayagen (1974), Social Feminists like Firestone (1970), Millett (1971) and Radical Feminists such as Deem Rosemary (1978) Kelly and Nihlen (1982) and Wolpe (1978) reveal the negative role played by the school system in reinforcing traditional patriarchal ideologies. They not only suggest the kind of curriculum that is needed for promoting women's equality but also suggest the kind of roles that teachers have to play in undoing the traditional dominant ideologies.

TOWARDS EXPERIENTIAL LEARNING FOR WOMEN

RENU BHARDWAJ

This chapter deals with the issue of gender and ways in which gender affects the outcome of learning in distance teaching institutions. It proposes ways of restructuring teaching strategies to relate them to women's lives and experiences so as to validate women as individuals and as a group as we are aware, "the socio-obscurantist conventions related to women's lives" (Bhardwaj, 1992, p. 32) have imposed a structure of education which is male-oriented and authoritative in nature. It is the special concern of feminist research to analyse women's learning in relation to this structure. There seems to be structural injustice in curriculum planning and teaching methodologies that deny women power, fair opportunities to develop their potential and work for a more just society.

This sexism is to be seen in the higher attrition rate. "Women have higher drop-out rates than men i.e. they are more affected by factors working against their continuation" (Prummer, 1988, p.57). Gender effects are visible also in the low enrolment rates (Annexure I). Though these can also be attributed to economic and geographically isolated conditions of women's placement and other factors, it remains to be seen whether a more general, non-sexist approach will help learning. After all the style of education connects with social movements. The only way education can serve the interests of women is if it is imparted in a democratic way to enable women's participation in decision-making so as to bring social change. The extraordinary success of the "consciousness raising techniques" (Spender, 1988, p.34) related to the women's movement provides testimony to the value and validity of experiential education which aims at cutting across traditional principles of pedagogy and realising the fundamental principle of education as self-actualisation. It has provided environment, opportunities and stimulus for individuals to grow as self-propelled inquirers of knowledge.

Women psychologists such as Belinky, Clinchy, Goldberger, Tarule (1986) and Carol Gilligan (1979) as also Piaget (1965) and Kohlberg (1981) based a study on adult women learning on moral reasoning, responsibility and care that govern learning. They studied women diverse in age and ethnic and socio-economic backgrounds as they discussed factors important about learning. Some of the principles drawn out from these studies are summed up by the Council of Adult Education in Melbourne as follows:

1. Women's experience and knowledge form the framework through which aspects of curriculum could be studied and evaluated.
2. Control of what is studied and how it is studied should be in the hands of the learners. Women have been denied such power in the past and need it for effective learning in the future.
3. Learning in groups and that too women only groups is a necessary factor in feminist learning. This frees women to focus on women's experiences, gives women space to develop education which is of most use to them, and eliminates prevailing structural oppression in mixed gender learning where, men commonly take up two-thirds of the time and attention available.
4. Mutuality of learners and teachers, the absence of competition and respect for the value of each woman's contribution are important characteristics of feminist learning principles.
5. The outcome of feminist learning being social justice, women are accountable to other women in shared awareness situations. This accountability would manifest in communication of insights thus gained and working towards a process of a more just society for all.

These precepts call for a fresh look at the design, facilitation and evaluation of learning for women, especially in distance education.

In 1983, the First International Council brochure on Experiential learning defined experience-based learning as that in which the learner is directly in touch with the realities being studied. It is contrasted with learning in which the learner only reads about, and talks or writes about these realities. Experience-based learning typically involves not merely observing the phenomena being studied, but also doing something with it; testing the dynamics of that reality to learn more about it, or applying the thing learned to achieve a more desired result. Experiential learning has not invited the attention of researchers in distance education because of the lack of proximity between the teacher and the taught. This is a misnomer as the material resources and the media are likely to be used much more effectively through this method of imparting education.

Though educational theorists have made various hypothetical models and methodologies of imparting experiential learning (Dewey, 1963, Boud, Keogh and Walker, 1985; Jarvis, 1987; etc.), Kolb's cyclical model of learning (Kolb,1974, p. 28) still remains widely accepted for its simplicity and scope (Fig.1).

According to Kolb, learning comprises the following stages.

- Concrete experience, followed by observation and reflection, which leads to
- the formation of abstractions, generalisations and hypothesis which require
- testing in new situations, thus giving rise to new experiences and the start of a new cycle.

What is important in Kolb's cycle is that experience without reflection, generalisation, hypothesis formation and testing does not result in learning. When all this occurs, experience becomes the best teacher. Reflective learning based on personal experience is an important paradigm in the feminist principles of learning. The Kolb model, though widely acclaimed, does not give specific instructions on how a teacher facilitator should manage a learning activity. It is Burch and Miller (1977) who developed an experiential model which suggests the kinds and sequencing of activities in such a way that a teacher can assist learners to reflect on their experiences and to generalise more effectively. This model, designs the learning activity into the following components (Fig.2):

Input Phase	preparing the learner for participation in the activity.
Activity	making the learner work through the activity according to the guidelines.
Processing Phase	converting the activity and experience of participation into individual's enquiry.
Generalisation Phase	moving from single concrete experiences to generalisations so as to develop concepts.
Next Input	testing out issues on the basis of common findings.

The first two stages of Burch and Miller's cycle i.e. the setting of the scene and the actual experiences have thin lines of demarcation. "The third stage is the most important and perhaps the most difficult to perform" (Ben Hart, 1978, p.75). It is during this stage that learners are helped to crystallise and internalise the learning which has occurred during the first two stages. But in distance teaching due to limitations imposed by the lack of proximity between the teacher and the taught, stage 4 of the cycle is as or rather more important. Whether behaviour has been modified or not has to be tested and ascertained at the 'Next Input' phase which coalesces with Testing Implication in new situations (Fig.1). Teaching assignments which are not part of the main body of learning but are sent separately can be made part of "Reflection-in-Action" which refers to the "interactive and interpretative skills exercised by a professional in the analysis and solution of problems" (Schon,

1987, p.iii). Teaching assignments can be the test of learning and should be made a part of the learning package.

A course in Social Sciences for example will aim to impress upon female students the differential effects of social and political environments on their lives. A skeletal assignment requiring them to identify a social problem, do research and develop a set of proposals and thus address the concerns that are most relevant to them can be improvised. This activity can be followed by observation and analysis which is supported by relevant readings.

Having made women struggle through their experiences, realising the limitations of their own socio-political postulates, we can help them to analyse the types of manipulations and coercion implicit in the traditional definitions of power and feminist notions of empowerment and liberation. Using gender as a category of analysis, we can ask questions relevant to the lives of an elderly woman, a divorced woman, a widow and to look at issues never considered relevant. Thus, in addition to social and political issues we could look at work in urban planning, architecture, environmental psychology to bring in a holistic approach to the study of the subject. Thus theoretical conceptualisations arrived at by reflective practices can be further tested out by personal data and a personal delineation of experiences within community boundaries. The conceptual segregation on the basis of economy can be illustrated when an economically weaker woman, a village learner, for instance contrasts the experiences with that of a city woman learner. These experiences can be supplemented by audio and video presentations by local officials or social workers. A study on local government can be made through an assignment which requires women to identify local representatives and conduct personal interviews. These interviews can be used to test the theories of representation explained in the units. This way they start seeing public officials as human and accessible and they may even aspire for these positions and roles.

To make self as a source of authority, assignments can either be planned to help women examine their daily living or to compose essays on what school was like and how it was like to grow up as a woman. These compositions can generate inner cues—insights into the gender role, socialisation and stratification and into the experience of power structures in different types of settings. The self-reflective components and action-oriented approach in the content planning can help forefronting issues which are rarely raised in such courses.

To make assignments relevant to the needs of women learners the following methods can be adopted:

1. Greater share of objective questions related to living sent alongwith course material and quick evaluation.
2. Evaluation of some portion of assignment through a healthy women-only group discussion.
3. Sample group discussion conducted by the counsellors as a feedback to course writers. Video and audio recordings of the major trends emanating from these discussions could be used as a stimulus for further 'reflection in action'.
4. Assignments designed to cater to the demographic profile based groups—data about the age, gender, educational level, reading skills, values, beliefs and vocational experiences analysed by the computers.
5. Introduction of computers for bringing in uniformity of evaluation and promoting exepriential learning to determine women biases and corrective measures through centrally devised floppies.

Thus starting off from Kolb and Burch and Miller Cycles of learning activities, distance teaching could embark on a whole range of activities such that are process-oriented as against linear mode of teaching and learning.

Last but not least is the issue of integrating women's experience in the curriculum - let us say in the discipline of English. Curriculum planners often add a single woman author to their otherwise male-dominated syllabi. What they need is to sense the importance of entirely reconceptualising these courses. English faculty's passionate devotion to the ideas of a literary canon - an eternally durable set of indisputable master pieces need to be challenged. Disciplines come to establish certain assumptions, principles, and methods as professionally legitimate. While planning the syllabi androcentric assumptions hold sway and often significant female writers are eliminated from the canon. Institutional as well as theoretical and historiographic factors are involved in such an exclusion. The prevailing assumptions of dominance and woman's subordination should be given up. Perhaps, a gender-balanced selection of writers can help the course give a regard commensurate with their numbers. Description of women as sexual objects seem to reflect D.H. Lawrence's own notorious libido. The best of psychological nuances and social observations may fail to provide insights that distinguish particular works by women. The writings to Kamla Markandaya, Alice Walker, Tony Morris, Doris Lessing, Kamala Das, Mary Susan, Roberta Sykes, Sylvia Plath view sexuality, motherhood, bodily appearance, marriage from a perspective that men cannot share. The relationship of feminine beauty to a woman's economic survival comes in sharp focus in Jane Austen's novels. Kamala Markandaya's narrative 'Nectar in a Sieve' suggests the possibility of male-female friendship as a force that can mitigate social evils.

Traditionally, literature courses emphasised three kinds of writing - fiction, poetry and drama and sometimes autobiography as well. But several women have turned to other types of writing, feeling inhibited or barred by public forms. Therefore, a determined effort is needed to rediscover women authors in journals, diaries, letters and even oral testimonies. Such writings can shimmer with evocative accounts of women's struggles to achieve self-awareness.

It would be far more profitable to consider feminist transformation of the curriculum and feminist pedagogy as conjugate perspectives, two sides of the same coin. Both these topics can be part of a single intellectual adventure.

REFERENCES

Belinky, Clinchy, Goldberger, Tarule (1986). *Women's Ways of Knowing: The Development of Self, Voice and Mind.* New York's Basic Books.

Bhardwaj, Renu (1992). 'Individual Existential Paradigm in Open Learning' in *A Collection of Papers from ISEL Publication,* Pondicherry, pp. 32-43.

Boud, D., Keogh, R.L.Walker, D. (1985). *Promoting reflection in Learning : A model.* London : Kogan Paul.

Burch, N. and Miller, K. (1977). *Teacher Effectiveness Training: Instructor Guide.* Chicago: Collier Books.

Dewey, J. (1938). *Experience and education.* London: Collier Macmillan.

Einstein, A. (1989). Process-oriented Adult Learning in N. Brookton et al. (ed.) *Quarterly Experience,* ACEE, August - 1989, No. 24, pp. 66-76.

Hart, Ben. (1988). 'An Application of Experiential Learning to Organisation Development in Higgs, J. (ed.) *A Collection of Contributions from ACEE Publication.* Sydney, ACED, pp 75-77.

Jarvis, P. (1987). Meaningful and meaningless experience: Towards an analysis of learning from life. *Adult Education Quarterly,* 37 (3) : 164-172.

Kolb, D. (1984). *Experiential Learning: Experience as the Source of Learning and Development.* New Jersey: Prentice-Hall.

Prummer, C.V. (1988). 'Women in Distance Education' in Daniel, J et al. (ed.) *14 ICDE Conference Papers,* Sweden, pp. 57-62.

Rich, Adrienne (1979). 'Claiming on Education'. *On Lies Secrets and Silence. Selected Prose 1966 - 1978* . New York: Norton.

Spender, L. (1988). 'Consciousness - Raising for Women in Experience based Learning in Higgs, J. (ed.) *A Collection of Contribution from ACEE Publication.* Sydney, ACED, pp 34-35.

ANNEXURE I

STATISTICS OF NEW ADMISSIONS - 1993
CATEGORY-WISE DISTRIBUTION

INDIRA GANDHI NATIONAL OPEN UNIVERSITY

Programme	Year	Total	Male	Female
BPP.B.A.	-	9265	6815	2450
BPP.B.Com.	-	2607	2235	372
B.A.	1st	9000	5896	3104
B.Com.	1st	3163	2421	742
B.Sc.	1st	1465	1229	236
B.A.	2nd	4477	2955	1522
B.Com.	2nd	1636	1243	292
B.Sc.	2nd	538	446	92
B.A.	3rd	2462	1800	882
B.Com.	3rd	826	627	199
BLS	-	1437	814	659
Management				
Fresh	-	8368	7516	852
Re-registration	-	5839	5663	176
SDM(DE)	-	11888	10894	994
DDE	-	485	303	182
DCE	-	574	321	253
DCO	-	853	731	122
DRD	-	2370	1738	632
DHE	-	938	593	345
CFN	-	5957	1086	4871
CIG	-	1081	328	753
MADE	-	188	158	30
DCH	-	213	164	49

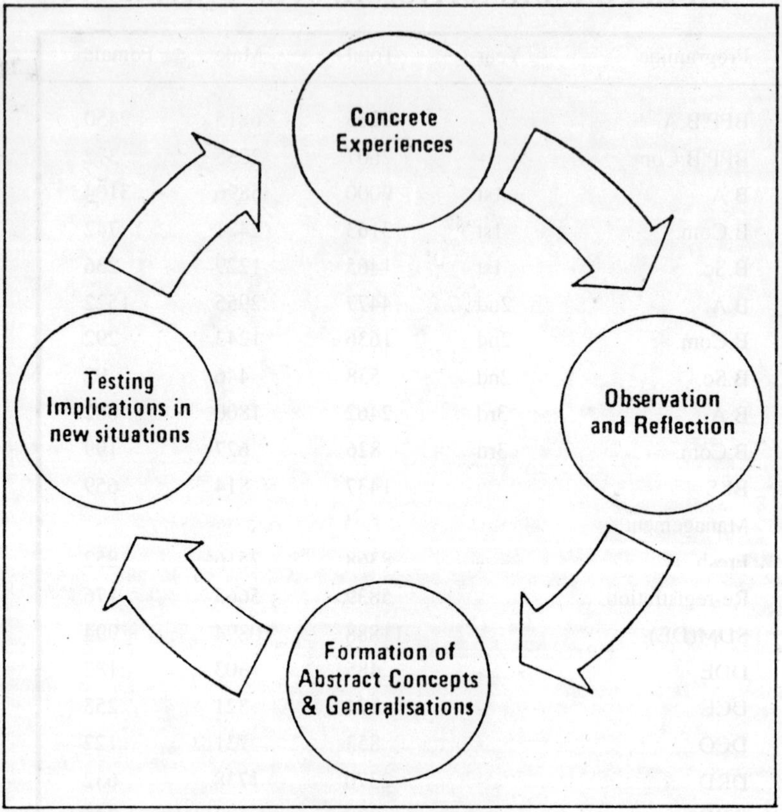

Fig. 1: Cyclical Model of Learning (Kolb et al., 1974, p. 28)

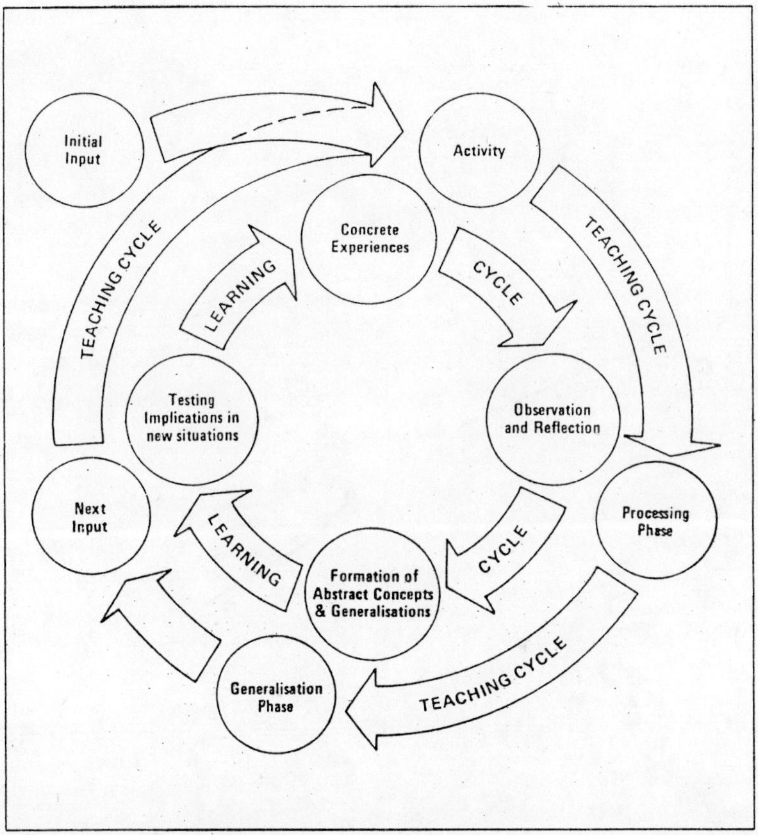

Fig. 2 Diagram showing the relationship between stages of the Kolb models of learning and Burch and Miller model of teaching.

REACHING OUT: THE ROLE OF COUNSELLING

C. PUSHPA RAMAKRISHNA

Counselling, Definition and Scope

Counselling, the Encyclopaedia of Education tells us, is the process of helping people to change their behaviour in the direction they choose. In any educational system today the focus is on the learner. As such, every institution must direct its efforts towards providing the best mix of objectives, methods and evaluative systems for the learner. However, very often the learner's reasons for enrolling in the course, her level of personal attainment, ambitions and the requirements of the course, work at cross-purposes creating a sense of insecurity. On such occasions counselling or guidance can be of direct help in understanding lessons, making a choice of subjects for social adjustment and for meeting the requirements of the course. In Distance Education, the term 'counselling' and the concept cannot be described as neatly or as succintly. The reasons are many. The teaching learning situations are different and so are the teachers and learners in these systems. The field and its processes are at an evolutionary stage and a certain degree of ambiguity attaches to them. Thus the 'counselling' of psychotherapy, vocational guidance cells and academic tutoring are all subsumed under the cover term 'counselling' as it is used in distance teaching institutions.

Distance Education and Counselling

Distance Education made its formal appearance in India in the early sixties but the idea of an Open University which provides greater opportunities for using various types of instructional modes, is of more recent origin. Within the latter system, there are different ways of reaching out to the learners - through printed course materials which are specially prepared in the self-instructional format, through radio-broadcasts, audio and video lessons; through letters and telephone calls; and by providing select occasions for direct communication with the Tutors, Counsellors or Co-ordinators at a study centre.

Distance education is a conceptually different form of study from conventional or formal education. Intended primarily for those who have not entered the conventional system, it must cater to a different set of learners. The differences are social, psychological and academic. Learners in this system are those who have been branded as 'socially disadvantaged' in having missed the opportunity for a formal education. These learners face many hurdles in re-starting their educational ventures and need constant support both moral and academic. Furthermore, the educational network in a distance teaching institution is such that it tends to look extremely complex to one who is not initiated into its working. This complexity of the system adds to the learners' bewilderment. Bureaucratic processes baffle the learner who is isolated from the institution and her peers and is unsure of herself. In response to felt needs arising from such an environment the university needs to make use of 'counselling' sessions. The institution thus renders a service to the learner to help her clarify her objectives, overcome difficulties of various sorts, and accept life in its many facets.

Education and Women

When we examine the role of education and women's relationship with it certain crucial issues are raised. Education has long been a means of exploitation of certain classes of society and on account of socio-cultural attitudes, women have been deprived of the opportunity for education. Whether it be in providing access to education or transfer of technology, the gender bias has prevailed and women have had a raw deal in India as in other countries, suffering from the impact of negative conditioning. Thompson (1983) speaking of women and adult education, shows how in the planning, design and production of courses, the focus has been on what is traditionally recognised as women's work i.e. childcare, beauty-care, household, food and nutrition, interior decoration and management of the house. The language used in courses for women has further reinforced such thinking. As a result, the traditional myths about women's roles and responsibilities have continued to weigh down upon them despite their exposure to higher education and development. Such conditioning causes latent complexes to surface when the learner experiences problems and has to take recourse to counselling.

Distance Education and Women

The distance learner in India, particularly the woman distance learner is no privileged student devoting her time to her study or her career interests only. She is surrounded by a multitude of academic and non-academic concerns. At the centre of the figure above is the woman learner surrounded in the immediate environment by such difficulties as are study-related. She may find the concepts difficult to understand and the language unintelligible. A gap in her educational background may also have created a certain degree of anxiety and reticence. She may lack the requisite study skills. Then she may experience more specific problems such as not knowing how to answer an assignment or feeling tense and worried before an examination. But, surrounding this area of the academic environment is the sphere of non-academic concerns. In addition to personal demotivating forces and lack of concentration, the student must face institutional problems such as delays in the receipt of materials and communication gaps, physical problems such as not having a suitable place to study in; problems related to her cultural ethos such as having to bear the burden of household responsibilities, the problems of the family, such as a child's ill-health etc. She may also not have the economic freedom to decide to start or continue her education, official or career-related work and a generally non-supportive attitude around her might make the woman distance learner's task more difficult than that of her male counterpart.

The socio-cultural environment around her is such that she labours under a complex if she takes time off for study. We can explain that this is on account of her unconscious acceptance of her roles in society as a woman and in her home as a parent as primary. Study is seen against such responsibilities as only a secondary priority which draws her away from her main task in life. Faith (1988) affirms this when she mentions that we need to "appreciate that many female students including those who are employed have primary or sole responsibility as parents" (p 78). The state of affairs in India is graver since the socio-cultural environment is much more traditional and the woman more "homebound" than women in the west.

Wherever there is a certain degree of liberation from traditional statuses regarding women and education, education is seen as a lesser evil and a safe diversion for women. Women, the men feel, are better occupied in study than in other recreations. Thompson (1983) discusses the idea that educational involvement is permitted for a woman only as a recreational avenue. It is only after attending to her housework, her husband and her children that she is permitted to turn to study, so much so that the advent of a guest is an immediate occasion for her to return to household work from which she had temporarily drawn herself away to attend tutorial sessions at the college.

Counselling for Women Distance Learners

Counselling in the educational context has been defined as the advice, help and support given to students to enable them to make satisfactory progress in this system. We shall relate this broad definition to the difficulties and pressures experienced by women distance learners and try to see how counselling can help them to progress satisfactorily towards their goals or at least arrive at a reconciliation between the complex roles in their lives.

In the Open University system counselling is of two types, group counselling and individual counselling. Group counselling could be organised both for academic and non-academic purposes:

- Study skills
- Clarification of doubts
- Discussion of salient points in lessons
- Study patterns
- Planning time

Academic Counselling

Weekend contact opportunities are provided to distance learners, in the Open Universities. These are primarily intended to be occasions for the clarifications of doubts and for interacting with one's counsellors and peers. The most common complaint of the counsellors who 'teach' at these sessions is that their learners do not ask for clarifications of doubts. The expectations of the learners are very different from those of the counsellors or academic tutors. There is a tendency on the part of learners to expect lectures on the subject rather than to make a prior reading of the text and to go to the counselling sessions to get particular points discussed. Women learners, particularly, are unable to take time off from their chores and read the lessons before attending counselling sessions. The need to critically read the lessons is also not felt. The main reason for this appears to be a lack of proper orientation to the role of the learner in this system. An assurance that the counselling session is a session where individual responses will be acceptable and welcome, needs to be made by the organiser of the session such that gradually preconceived notions of teacher and taught give way to a counseller-learner relationship where sharing and caring are the key words. In the case of women, group tutorial sessions for academic support are marked by similar issues as had been mentioned above:

(1) inhibitions regarding attending such sessions arise due to reasons which are often non-academic e.g. age, shyness on account of gap in study;
(2) fear, diffidence regarding one's own abilities;
(3) lack of means of expression often because of reduced exposure to such environments;

(4) feeling of disorientation in the strange surroundings, lack of a sense of belonging.

Such attitudes often come in the way of study patterns and need careful and discrete handling. Once the counsellor establishes a rapport with the learners and helps them face their problems squarely, they can become quite competent at individualized study.

Non-academic Group Counselling

In the experiences recounted by Carl Rogers (1983) the group counselling mode is used for establishing better links with learners and helping them in overcoming their personal problems. Rogers (1983) describes the strategies employed in non-academic group counselling "encounter" sessions. Such sessions, however, may not be suitable for the conditions prevailing among women distance learners in India. Here indiviual counselling would be more appropriate particularly in view of socio-cultural attitudes and the unconsciously developed biases. Socio-cultural taboos prevent learners from meeting in a group and discussing matters which are personal. Thus a group encounter is very uncommon for non-academic counselling or guidance. Women learners do not externalise their personal concerns or even admit them to themselves. Cases such as the ones cited by Kamala (1989) where the women distance learners are under pressure from members of their family to discontinue their studies are not uncommon. It is however quite rare for a counsellor to get an opportunity to approach and counsel members of the students' family. Thus group counselling for more or less generalisable concerns and individual counselling for personal problems would seem to be the most appropriate.

*Case Studies**

In order to illustrate exactly how women learners with either general

* *Note : These case studies have been developed from interviews and communications with actual students of the undergraduate and postgraduate courses of APOU and IGNOU.*

or specific problems reach out to the institution or its representative and vice versa, at this stage, I propose to recount some case studies.

Case study - 1

Mrs. Jasbir: " I was brought up in a very conservative atmosphere. We were practically kept 'underground'. Our house had large basements where women, particularly unmarried women, had to stay all the time. We were not allowed to speak loudly or walk with a hasty step. The bangles we wore had to be tight so that the jingling sound could not be heard by the men outside. For eighteen years I lived in such conditions in my father's house learning only the 'womanly' qualities—cooking and feeding the men and looking after the house. I came to this city when I was twenty (that too by chance - I had to help my sister during her delivery because my mother could not leave the house and go to attend on her)."

Mrs. Jasbir is a fifty-two year old student of the undergraduate course. She is an excellent cook and makes pickles and chutneys most effortlessly. Five years ago, her children (three of them, one a manager in a reputed firm, the other an engineer and the third, a daughter studying for M.D.) persuaded her to join the Open University. But her confidence had been eroded by her upbringing and her environment. She says "I can't go on! I'm far too old to study. I just can't remember anything. After all, I don't want to take up a job or anything. Maybe I should just give up studies or limp through them taking one exam at a time".

Case study - 2

Mrs. Meena is a young and energetic lady. She had enrolled herself in a conventional college but could not attend classes regularly because she had to stay at home to look after her three-month old son. This year her mother has enrolled herself in the BA Programme of the Open University through the non-formal stream, Mrs. Meena wonders if she too can join this 'new' type of University where attendance is not compulsory and she can do other things.

Ms. Meena: "Madam, do you think that I can join your University? I am just not able to attend classes at the college, I'm falling short of attendance ... and then, I want to join my husband in the States in another two years. I want to learn computer languages and typing also in that time. And, I may even have to leave at short notice and come to take the examination later ... Can you help me, please?"

Case study - 3

Counselling through correspondence:

Learner to Counsellor

Dear Madam,
I'm sorry to trouble you, but, do you mind if I write to you from time to time? I stay so far away and we don't get any news of developments there. Sometimes I don't even receive letters from the University in time!

My examination registration form, for example. I could only barely manage to send in the registration form before the last date. When I wrote to the Examination Branch they told me I should have watched out for the newspaper notifications. How can I? I stay in another State and don't get the local newspapers so, please, can I write to you or speak to you over the phone?

Case study - 4

Counselling through correspondence: Counsellor to Learner:

Dear Ms. Lakshmi,
I have gone through your second assignment and am glad that you have made considerable improvement. Congratulations, Your elaboration of the points on page 4 and your examples to illustrate them are also good. The only suggestion I have to make is that you could have organised your ideas more carefully mentioning the general ones first and then gone on to the detailed elaboration of each. Had

you done so you could have secured a higher grade. For the present, I can only award you a 'B' grade. I do hope you will bear my suggestions in mind the next time. Wishing you all the best.

Case study - 5

Mrs. Rashmi is a fairly confident-looking lady who has bravely shouldered the responsibilities of her family of three after an unfortunate separation from her husband. She has painstakingly gone through the undergraduate course and has successfully completed her postgraduate teacher-training programme. For advice in her personal, professional and academic concerns she turns to the counsellor in whom she hopes to find not just a guide and mentor but also a friend to share her joys and sorrows.

"I want your prayers, Madam, I have to undergo an emergency operation" she pleads. "I wanted you to be the first to know - I've got a new job".

Hello,
Madam, I called to ask you for some advice. Do you think I should enrol as an external student for the P.G. Programme of the University? Do you think it will improve my career prospects?

Identifying Areas for Counselling:

If we analyse these cases to identify the problems faced by the students and their need for counselling we would come up with a set of lists of the kind given below:

Case study - 1

1. Low self-esteem
2. Lack of confidence because of advancing age and a reduced academic exposure
3. Anxiety regarding examinations
4. Conditioning about failing memory
5. Inadequate or improper study skills.

The counsellor here would have to function mainly as a psychotherapist does. She would have to revise the learner's opinion of her own abilities, and suggest ways of improving her study skills such as making notes, using non-textual means for retention of details etc. Some counselling about time-planning and pacing of study could also help. A relationship of friendly concern and guidance about prioritizing her concerns will help the learner overcome her pre-conceived notions of age and failing memory.

Case study - 2

1. Non-formal type of education is attractive because it has fewer restrictions in terms of time and place of study.
2. Desire to be a part-time learner because of social, domestic and other commitments.
3. Desire to use the system at her own convenience, take examinations when she wants to.

Here, the subject is a prospective distance learner who is attracted to the idea of an education which does not place restrictions of time and place. The counsellor's function in this case will be largely one of a representative of the institution who familiarizes the entrant with the scheme of operations. A clear knowledge of rules and regulations and the ability to communicate them is what would be required of the counsellor.

Case study - 3

1. The learner is far away from the institution, and faces the isolation of a distance learner.
2. Desire to feel part of a system and institution.
3. Bureaucratic set-up baffles the individual.
4. Inability to cope with normal delays in a large organisation.
5. A non-urgent contact is desired for a reassuring and encouraging feeling.

This learner experiences some of the common problems of distance learners. She needs the reassurance that the institution cares for her and will assist her in her study. The bureaucratic machinery which expects her to follow the rules to the letter could demotivate her. The counsellor would have to play the role of a friend and guide who is approachable and who will if need be, protect the interests of her subject representating her case sympathetically to the institution.

Case study - 4

This is the comment received by the learner on an assignment response. Here the counsellor has done the following things:

1. Acknowledged the positive features of the work.
2. Established a personal communication.
3. Explained the grade given.
4. Evaluated the work in terms of other such responses.
5. Graded the answer.

Here the counsellor's comment on an assignment response establishes the conditions for a personal dialogue. At the same time she provides the learner an insight into the specific requirements of the assignment. She provides the "bench marks" (Sewart,1987) for the learner to assess herself and offers encouragement for the positive features of the work done.

Case study - 5

1. A case of post-programme counselling where guidance is desired
2. Need for a friendly word of assurance
3. Desire to share her moments of joy or tribulation

Here, again, the counsellor plays the role of advisor and friend but also provides the learner an opportunity to unburden herself in moments of grief. Though she may not be able to provide solutions or remedies, the counsellor can show concern by listening to the learner patiently and expressing warmth and sympathy.

Patterns of Response in Counselling

As has been mentioned above there are two main types of counselling—individual counselling and group counselling. These cover a wide range functions and could be grouped under tutoring, counselling or advising and giving information.

Tutoring or Study-related Counselling

Tutoring is study-related and includes activities such as: suggesting ways and means of improving one's reading skills, planning and designing assignments and projects, explaining the conventions of the subject, giving the salient points of a lesson how to revise it, and generally inducing the newcomer into the discipline and into its intricacies as well as providing an exposure to improved study skills. This form of counselling is most desired by non-formal students in the first year of their study. It is however put to use through the entire course of the student's tenure in the university.

Advising or Non-academic and Personal Guidance

This activity is largely learner-dependent and such cases need extremely careful handling. The counsellor will have to suggest different remedies to different clients depending on their personal qualities and the nature of their problems. The Rogerian 'non-directive' form of counselling would be most appropriate in such situations where the questions are as varied as the students themselves and very often the student resolves her own crisis by self-examination. It is possible to classify the problems of Indian women learners studying through the distance mode into the following categories:

Attitudinal problems: the role of women in society, their responsibilities and the clash be-

	tween these and personal ambitions.
Insitutional problems:	demotivating features of studying alone as part-time learners after a break in their education, delays in communication etc.
Study-related problems:	Lack of concentration, due to heavy responsibilities at home, inadequate exposure to academic conventions.

In the case of women learners the attitudinal problems such as the role of women in society, in the home etc., are so pervasive that they influence study patterns and even institutional problems. "Are the sacrifices that I and those around me make worth the possible (but not assured) benefit?" the letter asks (Thompson, 1983, p. 77). For instance, Ms. Veena says "I haven't received my course material yet but I don't know how I can go and enquire about it—I am so tied down by housework during the day". Ms. Veena's problem is, "I come from an orthodox family. They will not let me go anywhere or write to anyone. In fact, they say why must you study at all? But I want to be an educated woman."

Distance learning institutions provide opportunities for student-based rather than institution-based study. But few learners, whether male or female, find the study-material adequate for all their purposes. This takes us to the question of "intermediaries" (Sewart, 1987). "Intermediaries" or counsellors are necessary in a system which teaches at a distance because the academic and psychological needs of each student cannot be met by pre-structured texts. The interactive process required is a complex one and requires a supportive atmosphere rather than just an element of support. Such an environment can best be created by a counsellor-counsellee interaction. It is a relationship between two or more individuals, between human beings who think, feel and act in special ways. Not all its features can be anticipated which is most necessary for a non-starter or underprivileged learner.

Can we plan and pattern counselling?

Counselling theory helps us to describe and explain what a counsellor observes about her interactions with her clients. It systematizes and simplifies the complexities of her observation. In order to evaluate current practices and to provide guidance and rationales for future practice we need to examine the concept more deeply.

Behaviourist theories would advise laying down of specific goals, diagnosis and precision of methods, and matching results with the performance criteria laid down. Humanistic psychology, on the other hand, relies on existential theories. It examines larger issues such as problems developing from complexes about life and death, guilt and suffering, commitment and responsibility, Rogers' non-directive theory of counselling is client-centred and descriptive in its approach.

Encounters with distance learners over the years have suggested that no predetermined principles can be followed in counselling. Each client and case is different from the other and must be handled as such. It is thus necessary to make descriptive analyses of counselling encounters to arrive at the functions of the counsellor and learner.

The Structure that Develops in a Counselling Session

Taking a cue from Rogers (1983) it is suggested here that generally, a pattern of the following nature develops in a counselling session involving a woman distance learner.

Turns taken at a counselling session

1. Initial generalities exchanged
   S - May I come in? I'm a student of ....
   C - Yes, ... do sit down.
2. Feelers sent out to gauge the degree of freedom
   S - I'm sorry .... I hope I'm not disturbing you.
3. Identification with learner and situation

C - Of course not ... I'm here to help you ... we all need some guidance at times ....

4. 'Safe' areas of concern

   S - I came to tell you that ... actually I haven't attended any counselling sessions ... I just don't get the time on weekends .... There's so much work at home ... and then my husband and children are also home on that day.

5. Patient hearing given - No attempt to prioritize issues yet.

   C - Yes, I can understand.

6. Gradual lowering of defences

   S - Well ... actually ... you know my problem is ....

7. Placing things in the right perspective/going deeper to specifics.

   C- Have you tried going through the course material? ... you know, you should plan your time ... I think you should try talking to them about this problem ....

8. Raising negative points about the mode of study-defensive attitude.

   S - I received the books too late ... the parcel was not even packed properly ....

   Your radio lessons are broadcast at such odd hours ....

9. Explanatory role-trying to work towards positive thinking.

   C - You're right, but tell me, what would be a convenient time?

10. Weighing the information.

    S - Yes, I suppose you're right ... I must also do something about ....

11. Conciliatory role

    C - I hope you now understand your role in this system. Will you then try to understand why ....

By examining such moves or turns in counselling encounters we may arrive at the qualities required of the counsellors. Some of these qualities are related to the attitude of the counsellor and can be developed by orienting counsellors to the changed situation in distance learning systems and women's education through them.

Others, such as skills of communication, can be developed by training in practical workshops and being on the job. With an open-minded approach and a geniune interest in helping the learner through her problems, the counsellor can be a useful means of encouraging a positive approach to education among women.

1. Patience to listen to the learner's problems, to tolerate disturbance.
2. Sincerity of purpose—a desire to be of assistance.
3. Recognition of the learner/subject as an equal.
4. Ability to empathise—to put herself in her place.
5. Complete familiarity with the rules, and regulations and practices of the institution.
6. Clarity of expression and communicative skills
7. Ability to direct learners towards a positive outlook to life, study and other matters in general.

Equality of Women through Distance Education

Distance education is built on the principle of providing equal opportunities to all the members of society. One section of the underprivileged of society are women. Education is intended to be used as an agent in bringing about change in the status of women (NPE, 1986). That is to say, distance education can also be an instrument through which equal opportunities are to be provided to women. To quote Ram Reddy (1986, p. 9) "I see a ray of hope for emancipation of women in the field of education through the Open University system. Open Universities have the potential to convert the ideal of women's education into a reality. No social taboos or purdahs or social customs can stand between this University and the willing women learners". But can providing opportunities alone solve all the difficulties for the development of women's education?

Looking Ahead

The Programme of Action (1986, pp. 104-105) clearly mentions four features of its strategy for bringing about a change in women's status:

1. to gear the entire education system to plan a positive interventionist role in the empowerment of women;
2. to promote Women's Studies as a part of various courses and encouragement to educational institutions to take up active programmes to further women's development;
3. to widen the access of women in programmes of vocational, technical and professional education;
4. to create dynamic managerial structures to cope with the targets envisaged.

Let us now relate these policy decisions to counselling and its role in distance education. Counselling can be a useful means of bringing about a change in traditional attitudes to women and education. Its contribution to the building up of a positive self image and developing self-confidence in the traditionally exploited women members of society is also immense. Other qualities it can help enhance are the ability to think critically, exercise freedom in decision making and encouraging leadership qualities in organising group activities.

In the area of vocational guidance too counselling can play a significant role. What is needed however is adequate publicity of women's programmes and placement and recruitment services for women. In the curricula and programmes too it is necessary to introduce developmental themes such as awareness building about their roles in society, banking and investment procedures, legal and technical services, entrepreneurial development etc.; which have been largely considered "male-areas of study". By using pre-enrolment counselling a larger section of women can be made aware of programmes into which they could enrol themselves so that they could be benefited socially and individually.

Another suggestion for enhancing the role of counselling and for acquiring the best results from it is to assign a fixed number of learners (subjects) to each counsellor for the duration of her study.

The example of the United Kingdom Open University could be emulated in providing a counsellor for non-academic matters and a tutor or 'academic counsellor' for study-related matters, at least where the need for counselling is expressed and help is sought. Such planning would both structure the task of the counsellor and reduce the degree of fuzziness that surrounds it.

Counselling Counsellors

A matter which requires urgent attention is the question of counselling counsellors. As in the case of learners and new entrants into the system, counsellors too need to be oriented to the special features of the distance mode of study. For counselling women too a counsellor needs careful guidance and exposure to the issues. Personal qualities of communication, adequate information and most important of all, the right attitude to the problem at hand, can go a long way in reducing the demotivating influences of studying at a distance.

In conclusion , we can reassert that counselling , whether it be academic or non-academic, group or individual, vocational guidance or counselling for self-awareness, is one of the essential ways of reaching out in the distance education system.

REFERENCES

Deighton, Lee. C. (ed) *The Encyclopaedia of Education*, Macmillan and Free Press.

Educational Technology (June 1990). *Distance education for Women's Development : Report of the Commonwealth Women Vice-Chancellor's Conference*, p 10.

Faith, Karlene (1988). 'Gender as an issue in Distance Education'. *Journal of Distance Education*, Vol.3, No.1, pp 75-79.

Indira Gandhi National Open University (1988). *Diploma in Distance Education, Course 4, Block- 3. Counselling.*

Kamala, B.V. (1989). 'Need and nature of counselling in Distance Education' Paper presented at the Regional Seminar on Distance Education, South India, Vijayawada, Sept 1989.

Koul, B.N. and Bhatt, Anita (1988). 'Counselling—Basic Concepts and Technology' Background Material for Orientation Programme (for restricted circulation) IGNOU.

Nagaraja, Bhargavi (1990). 'The Gender bias in technology transfer', *The Hindu Sunday*, July 8.

Programme of Action, *National Policy on Education* 1986, New Delhi: Government of India.

Reddy, G. Ram (1986). 'Women's Education and Open University' Paper presented at 1st Convocation of Sri Padmavathi Mahila Viswavidyalaya, Tirupati.

Rogers, Carl (1983). 'The Process of the Encounter Group' in Education for Adults, Vol.1, *Adult Learning and Education* (ed) Malcolm Tight, Croomhelm and The Open University, London, pp 203-211.

Sewart, David (1981). 'Distance Teaching: A Contradiction in Terms?' in *Teaching at a Distance,* Vol-19, pp 8-18.

Thompson, Jane (1983). 'Women and Adult Education' in Education for Adults - Vol II *Educational Opportunities for Adults* (ed) Malcolm Tight, Croomhelm and The Open University, London.

SUPPORT SERVICES AND WOMEN : A CASE STUDY OF IGNOU STUDENTS IN KARNATAKA AND GOA

MANJULIKA SRIVASTAVA

The development and maintenance of student support services is of vital importance to distance education. IGNOU has a range of student support services that include providing learning materials to students, arranging contact programmes and conducting examinations. Student support services at IGNOU are carried out from the Headquarters, Regional Centres and Study Centres. Although the headquarters decides the policies and the modalities of student support services, the major work has to be carried out by the study centres. Regional Centres are the intermediary links between study centres and the headquarters. Study centres are the immediate points of contact for the students. Through its network of study centres and regional centres IGNOU provides both academic and administrative support to its distance learners.

As of October 1994, there are 16 Regional Centres located mostly at State capials and 229 study centres throughout the length and breadth of the country. To further extend support services the University has adopted a more flexible approach in the establishment of recognised study centres and sub-centres. This approach is expected to improve the outreach of the student support services to geographically remote areas. Every district is expected to have the services of at least one study centre by 1995 [Status Report of IGNOU, 1989]. The support services offered by the headquarters, regional centres and study centres are given below in Table 1.

TABLE 1
SUPPORT SERVICES

STUDY CENTRES	REGIONAL CENTRES	HEADQUARTERS
General Information	Information Centre	Attending to Student queries
Sale of Application forms	Students' admissions	Distribution of Self Instructional Materials & Assignments
Tutoring & Counselling	Collection of Fees	Evaluation of Computer Marked Assignments
Audio Visual & Library facilities	Reimbursement of Fees for SC/ST	Terminal evaluation
Computer Terminals & labs	Attending to Student Queries	Overall Grading
Student's continuous Evaluation (Tutor Marked Assignments	Maintenance of Student records	Declaration of Results
Conducting Term end exams		Awarding of Degrees/ Diplomas/ Certificates
Attending to Students' queries.		

This paper will focus on the following issues:

- Utilisation of support services by women students enrolled at Bangalore Study Centre;
- their satisfaction with the support services offered by IGNOU;

- suggestions to improve the support services to make them more effective and suitable for women students.

Women students enrolled at Bangalore Study Centre of the 1990-91 batch for Diploma in Computers in Office Management (DCO), Bachelors of Library and Information Science (BLS), Diploma in Management (DIM), Certificate in Food and Nutrition (CFN), were identified. A structured questionnaire with a few open-ended questions was sent to all of them. All the questionnaires received were considered for analysis. Interviews with women students were also conducted at the Bangalore Study Centre during counselling sessions to corroborate the information given by the respondents and also to get additional information.

The Bangalore Study Centre, attached to Bangalore Regional Centre, has the highest number of women students in the region enrolled for women's programmes. The details of enrolment of women students (1990-91 batch) at the other centres which are attached to the Bangalore Regional Centre are given in Table 2.

TABLE 2
ENROLMENT OF WOMEN AT BANGALORE REGIONAL CENTRE

Study Centre	DCO	BLS	DIM	CFN
Bangalore	1	35	17	25
Mangalore	*	*	1	4
Dharwad	*	*	1	4
Gulbarga	*	*	*	6
Goa	*	9	Nil	Nil

Women students of only four programmes have been selected as the eligibility requirements for all four programmes is different. Therefore women from different age groups educational backgrounds and employment status could be studied.

Women constitute 18% of the students enrolled at Bangalore Study Centre for the above programmes. The percentage of women's enrolment in two programmes is very high : 43% in CFN and 43% in BLS. However in DCO and DIM it is barely 5% and 6% respectively. Of these women students 85% are residents of urban areas and 15% are rural. The number of employed women is also very high : 67%, 4% of them being self-employed with only 29% being unemployed.

TABLE 3
PROGRAMMEWISE RESPONDENTS

PROGRAMME	QUESTIONNAIRES SENT	QUESTIONNAIRES RECD
DIM	17	9
DCO	1	1
BLS	35	12
CFN	25	12

88% of the women r`spondents are in the age group of 20 to 40 years. Only 6% are below 20 years of age and the remaining 6% fall in the category of 50 years and above. It is interesting to note that 50% of them are married and 50% unmarried. 82% of them are graduates and barely 12% are non-graduates. Only 18% are unemployed. 80% have met the expenses of the programme from their own salaries.

Utilisation of Support Services Offered by IGNOU

Course Material: The course materials that are prepared by IGNOU and sent to its students aim to stimulate independent learning. 82% of the women students received the course material as per schedule. Since all of them have submitted more than 50% of the assignments, it is obvious that they have gone through the course materials. Only 12% of the students (4 students of BLS programme) found the course material difficult, while all the others found it self-explanatory and easy to understand.

Audio/Video Programmes: Audio/Video Programmes are prepared by IGNOU to supplement the printed materials. These programme•

are telecast on National Network thrice a week besides being available to the distance learners at the study centres. 79% of the respondents found the audio video programmes good. Since 53% have not been able to see the video programmes broadcast on National network, most have seen them at the study centre.

Counselling: Counselling or periodic face-to-face interaction with academic counsellors and co-learners is held at study centres. It is the only way of clarifying personal needs, reconciling conflicting demands of home and work, and coming to terms with isolation and previous experiences of distance learners. 68% of the respondents have attended more than 50% of the counselling sessions scheduled for their programme.

The two major reasons given by married women for attending less than 10% of the counselling sessions are living more than 70 km from the study centre. They find it difficult to reach the study centre because of the distance. Interestingly, all the three candidates are from rural areas and are unmarried. The two major reasons given by married women for not attending counselling sessions regularly are (a) family duties and (b) demands of full time employment. Barely 6% of the students found the sessions a waste of time and therefore attended only 25% of the sessions. Table 4 gives the pattern of attendance programmewise.

TABLE 4

PATTERN OF ATTENDANCE AT COUNSELLING SESSIONS

Prog.	below 10%	11 to 25%	26 to 50%	50 to 70%	71 & above
DIM	1	-	-	3	5
DCO	-	-	-	-	1
BLS	2	2	2	-	6
CFN	-	-	4	-	8

(absolute numbers)

Library facilities: At all study centres, reference books are available for distance learners. All the students have visited the library but only 15% have actually made use of the library facilities. The reasons given by the remaining 85% are (a) insufficient reference books or non-availability of books; (b) no lending facility and (c) no time to refer to books after attending counselling sessions.

Evaluation: Assignments form a major component of the distance mode of education. It is one of the devices used to keep up continuous interaction with distance learners. Through assignments the institution gets the feedback, it not only assesses the learning of the students but also the effectiveness of the instructional materials. The tutor comments written by the counsellor on the evaluated assignments give a feedback to the distance learner on her performance, her understanding of basic concepts and on how to improve and correct the mistakes made by her with regard to her. All the respondents have submitted assignments and all except for two students of CFN programme did not get back their evaluated assignment responses.

All of them were satisfied with the periodicity of term-end examinations and 79% with the number of assignments for their programme. 21% want more assignments which is given in Table 5.

TABLE 5

OPINION ON NUMBER OF ASSIGNMENTS

Prog.	More	Less	No change
DIM	-	-	9
DCO	1	-	-
BLS	-	-	12
CFN	6	-	6

Effectiveness of Support Services

Self Instructional Materials

The students were asked to specify the number of times there was a delay in receipt of study materials and the inconvenience they faced thereof. Only 18% did not receive the study materials on time. It is clear that these students did not complete their assignments on time because of delayed receipt 12% of the respondents found the material difficult. They are all enrolled for the BLS programme. They would prefer the material to be in their regional language and suggested that the language used should be and more concise and simple.

Audio-Video Programmes

For more effective use of audio-video programmes some of the students suggested that the cassettes linked to the blocks should be shown in counselling sessions rather than a few cassettes being clubbed together in one session. Secondly 18% of the students found the audio programmes of a very low standard. Those students who could not view the telecasts on the national network have not been able to do so because of it being an early morning transmission. They would all prefer an evening slot on Doordarshan.

Counselling

The timings of counselling sessions suit all women students except for 6% of the DIM students who would prefer evening time on weekdays. 41% were not satisfied with the performance of the academic counsellors. They felt that they were not well-versed in the content of the study materials.

Evaluation

82% students find the time allotted for writing the assignments insufficient. 47% were dissatisifed with the tutor comments written on their assignments and 47% were satisfied, 6% did not receive their evaluated assignment responses. The major reasons given for their dissatisfaction are: (a) no comments (64%); (b) poor comments (29%) and (c) biased comments (7%).

Suggestions for Improving Effectiveness

The success of IGNOU depends to a large extent on the effectiveness of the support services being offered to its distance learners specially the women students. Housewives, working women and women in general form one of its major target groups. In order to develop a more responsive delivery system it is required to establish delivery networks at the regional level to meet the specific local requirements.

The library is an essential part of any educational programme. The university can launch a scheme of lending against deposit. Photocopying facilities at study centre libraries would also solve the problems of most distance learners, particularly women, who cannot spare much time after attending counselling.

For students, in particular women students living in remote areas or far away from the centre, the University should provide an alternative by organising intensive counselling once in 3 months instead of sessions spread over the whole year. It can also provide tutorial support through mobile counselling vans carrying IGNOU's course materials audio/video equipment and counsellors on fixed days.

More time on the national network (Doordarshan) for telecasts of its video programmes would be beneficial to its students. Similarly broadcasts of its audio programmes through AIR can be expanded. Most women preferred evening rather than morning transmissions as in the mornings they are fully occupied with cooking, getting children ready for school, and other household chores that need to be attended to.

As this study shows, most women prefer daytime counselling on holidays, IGNOU should continue with the same pattern. The attendance percentage is also very high among women students. The women students who were interviewed at counselling sessions expressed the need to attend counselling. Some of the reasons mentioned by them are: to learn more, to go through the SIMs with co-learners, to clarify doubts, to discuss the assignments with the counsellor, to meet fellow students, to keep in touch with the University.

More practical sessions for BLS and DCO courses should be introduced. Periodic workshops should be conducted for the academic counsellors relating to evaluation techniques and skills of counselling as some of the respondents were not satisfied with the tutor comments and the performance of the counsellors. All state governments should follow the example set by the Gujarat State Government by giving full-fee reimbursement to women students. This step would encourage more women to enrol for higher education and benefit from the courses offered by IGNOU.

S.N.D.T. WOMEN'S UNIVERSITY AND DISTANCE EDUCATION

UMA VANDSE

The inauguration of the first Indian Women's University on June 3, 1916 marked the emergence of a new era in the history of women's education in the country. In 1920, Sri Vithaldas Thackersay announced a magnificent donation of Rs. 15,00,000 in memory of his mother. As per the condition laid down by the donor, the University came to be known as Shreemati Nathibai Damodar Thackersay Women's University or SNDT as it is now generally known.

Special Features

SNDT introduced the following principles on which the curricula was to be based :

(1) Mother tongue as a medium of instruction in Higher Education.
(2) To facilitate the students to have a free subject choice as per their capacity and the social needs.
(3) To plan such courses which will enable women to discharge better their familial obligations.

If we look at these features critically, it can be seen that they are progressive as they focus on imparting instruction to the learner's capacity, and the necessity of an education that is relevant to life.

Maharshi Karve (founder of the university and prominent social worker who worked for the upliftment of Indian women) had designed the educational programme for women based on their perceived responsibilities which were different from those of men.

But the different nature of the curricula for women generated the feeling that the education offered by the Women's University was substandard.

Objectives of the Women's University

(1) To inculcate the feeling of responsibility and self-confidence in women in order to be at par with men.
(2) To educate them to become better housewives in order to develop better family ties.
(3) To instill in women the spirit of nationalism and deep reverence for distinguished scholars, patriots and learned women.
(4) To educate the women who wish to follow a career.

Out of the above four objectives three were the fundamental principles in the educational planning of the Women's University suitable to those times. The first objective was universal and the second and third were for housewives and mothers. The fourth one was a little different in nature as it was solely for career women. In view of this objective Maharshi Karve said:

> The intelligent women can avail of the education from our University and expand their knowledge to any extent and offer their services for the welfare of the society.

Reactions of the Society

There was a mixed feeling in the society regarding the objectives of this University. The first point of contradiction was regarding the very need of a separate education for women. The social consensus was against women's education and specially the idea of providing higher education to women evoked bitter criticism. Social scholars like Dr. Natarajan also opposed the idea of a women's university. The Committee appointed for the improvement of Bombay University also expressed a similar opinion (1924). According to them a separate university for women was a sheer waste of money and time.

The use of the mother tongue as a medium of instruction in higher education also brought forth criticism. There was no place for mathematics in the curriculum and this was also a ground for criticism. The Radhakrishnan Commission had made it clear that there is a need of different courses for women, since men and women fulfil different obligations and functions in life and that home science and domestic science were specially suited to women. Dr. Karve and others thought that women should study some special subjects like Home Science and Fine Arts. Optional subjects included Mathematics, Physics, Chemistry, Sanskrit, Hindi, Drawing, Music and even French and German. These subjects had a great practical value in the life of a girl. This was the third special feature of the University.

A remarkable characteristic of this University was its all-India jurisdiction. Dr. Karve felt that a women's University for Maharashtra only was too narrow a project if the target was to provide facilities for higher education to girls from all over India. With this view the University was named 'Bharatvarshiya Mahila Vidyapeeth' (All India Women's University). The Entrance Examination even at that time was held in Marathi, Gujarati, Sindhi and Telugu. And the medium of instruction at college level was Gujarati, Marathi and Sindhi.

Bearing in mind the paucity of colleges, and also the social conditions discouraging women from receiving higher education, half a century ago, it was Dr. Karve's view that unless private candidates were allowed to appear in the university examinations, women's education would make no substanital progress. By allowing private candidates to appear in the University exams, the University also took care to see that standards did not fall. Today, when Distance Education has become popular all over the world, it would be well to remember that this idea was nursed and nurtured first in India by SNDT through its practice of examining private candidates.

In 1936, the headquarters of the University were shifted from Pune to Bombay. The Nursing Department was established as a department of the S.N.D.T. College for Women, Bombay, introducing the degree courses in Nursing. The same year the B. Ed. department was established as a department of the S.N.D.T. College for Women and in 1959 the university established the Home Science department which was later converted into a full-fledged college. People have begun to realise that Home Science does not mean only cooking, laundering or dressmaking. It has a richer content, a deeper meaning and rests on the philosophy which has great significance in the context of the world today. It is education which teaches the art of healthy living, living within one's means and in harmony within the family and within the community. The Home Science college students for their undergraduate and post-graduate studies make use of 22 well-equipped laboratories including Nursery schools, Home Management Residence flats and Research laboratories for advanced studies. Areas of specialisation are Child Development, Food and Nutrition, Textile and Clothing, Family Resource Management, Home Science Extension Education. (See Annexure 1 for facultywise courses at SNDT).

Academic Activities

The Department of Continuing and Adult Education was established in 1971 in response to the U.G.C. call for non-formal education programmes. This department offers a variety of opportunities for women either to add to their knowledge and skills, or to continue their interrupted education. The department also consciously strives to help women acquire an understanding of the altered social milieu and their rights and obligations as citizen. Its target group covers a broad spectrum of the population stretching from illiterate slum dwellers to educated women including practising professionals. Courses offered to the former range from routine literacy and numeracy, to simple but rich courses in nutrition, child-care, health care, legal rights awareness, etc. Other courses include interior design, textile design, journalism, marriage counselling, dealing with drug addiction, computer application, entrepreneurship, etc.

The Research Centre for Women's Studies was started in 1974 with a view to expanding and strengthening its activities. In 1980 the University Grants Commission accorded it the status of a Centre for Advanced Research in Women's Studies. The Centre has three major thrusts—documentation, research and training. The documentation unit has rich resource material on women and brings out selections and translations. It is building a South Asia network and is presently engaged in computerising its collections. Research is the core activity of the Centre. The Centre has collaborated with several national and international agencies, e.g. CSIR, ICSSR, NCERT, UNICEF, UNESCO, UNDP. A number of publications have been brought out by the Centre.

Women in Distance Education

The Distance Education system is a new concept in the rapidly developing world of education. India is one of the pioneering countries of the developing world which found in the system of distance education a suitable answer to the fast-growing educational needs of the country. Thus the system of external education has existed in S.N.D.T. Women's University since the last 50 years. Maharshi Karve had thoroughly studied the status and situation of Indian women. It was rather impossible for women—especially girls to come out of their homes and attend the classes in the formal education system. Hence, he took education to their doorsteps. Correspondence Courses were started in the year 1961 in India to provide a parallel system to the formal system of education, as a remedy for the problem of the growing demand for formal education. The underlying principle of Distance Education was that it should be mainly for deprived sections of society namely, the rural youth, women and the employees in the government and non-government institutes: In S.N.D.T. Women's University though the external degree education was possible for women it had some constraints. The learners were studying in isolation without any material for guidance. The emergence of correspondence courses offered one more facility to get the reading material i.e. the printed notes at home. Now Distance Education provides reading material, personal contact lectures, tutorials, feedback and audio facility. Such advancement in the system encouraged women to aspire for higher education. Though this facility has straightaway entered the kitchen, the number of women in higher education is still very negligible i.e. only 1% of the total student population in Higher Education.

The Department of Correspondence Courses and Distance Education at SNDT was established in the year 1979 when Dr. Madhuriben Shah was the Vice-Chancellor. Dr. Madhuriben a renowned educationist has said in "Challenges to Higher Education in Changing India":

> A University is meant to be an institution of acquisition and dissemination of knowledge and for fostering free and responsible thinking. While discharging this function, it releases forces for harnessing the capability of youth and for taking humanity onwards in its march of self knowledge and self expression.

After 1979, thousands of women completed their degrees. The Department started with a humble enrolment of 784 and the latest enrolment figure is over 12,000. But this number is insignificant in comparison with the female population of the country. Why this imbalance in the ratio of women learners ? When we look at the issue, we see that socio-economic conditions are the root cause for this state of affairs.

Survey in Distance Education

The Survey conducted by the Department of Distance Education of the S.N.D.T. Women's University reflects many vertical and horizontal trends of women's education which promote or demote women's education.

The survey reveals that the Distance Education Programme has become more popular in urban areas rather than semi-urban and rural areas. The ratio of working to non-working students of the department also tilts more towards working women. When we look at the size of the family from where the learners have come, it shows that learners from medium-sized families are more inclined towards Distance Education. The respondents who were taking advantage of the courses were mostly employed in low income groups (primary school teachers, nurses, clerks). One-third of the total respondents were in the income group of Rs. 2,000/- per month. The data have also revealed that in nearly 50% of the families, there is only one earning member. Regarding the payment of the fees, the data show that the students pay their fees from their own earnings, or in a few cases, from the family income while a few from the aid given by social-religious institutions. The data regarding the attitude of the families and society show that the attitudes are more or less encouraging.

The survey has given a deep insight into the development of Distance Education for women. In personal interviews the women were very vocal regarding their aspirations and expectations. The Distance Education programme receives no financial assistance from any source. The programme is fully dependent on the registration fees collected from the students. As such no financial assistance is rendered by the university. As per the principle of S.N.D.T. University the reading material is prepared in four languages so the major share of the fees collected is spent on printing materials. The University cannot afford to give any financial aid either to the economically backward women or to the socially backward. Highly motivated women could not continue their education due to economic dependence. If supported financially, every third woman in the country is interested in availing herself of the second chance for education. This is a vital issue as far as Distance Education in the country is concerned.

Another unpleasant condition of distance education for women is that of age limits at the entry level. As per the U.G.C. guidelines the learner should be of age 21 plus. In case of women learners, specially girls, this eligibility condition is very unfortunate. Generally the girls complete their secondary education by the age of 17-

18. As per our patriarchal family pattern the boy in the family gets encouragement for higher education. So the girl who has completed her secondary education has to suffer stagnation in life. If this age limit is lowered for the girls, to the age of 18, they would be able to fulfil their dreams of gaining higher education.

The Distance Education system is basically an encouraging factor for women in a few other respects. In case where families do not allow the widow to freely move in society often allow them the option of enroling in Distance Education institutions. It is observed that the social problems in society are changing with the change in time. For years together widowhood was a major problem in society. Today this problem has been replaced by the problem of destitutes. This number is on the increase. Social evils like dowry are still prevalent in the society. As such many victims of the dowry system are coming forward to higher education through the distance mode. In Gujarat State—specially in Saurashtra, I met many such students who were benefited by this system. According to them this second chance of education in life is a sort of rebirth.

Not only degree education but job-oriented courses should be developed in the Distance Education system. These courses can make women self-reliant. These courses can be arranged for different categories of society as per their needs. Till today, women require guidance in different aspects of personality development. These courses should be designed to suit different economic groups as well as regional, geographical backgrounds. For this purpose a national level survey should be conducted by the National Open University. This survey will give us a real insight into the development of Distance Education Programmes for women. But for the implementation of such schemes there is no infrastructure, no financial aid.

What SNDT hopes to Achieve in Future

Today SNDT strives to call for five distinct thrusts:

(1) To provide education to girls and women whose access to

it is limited or poor. This includes those who are located in remote areas, those who belong to families who do not yet recognize the need to educate women, those whose schooling or university education has been cut short by marriage, motherhood or other contingencies, those who are restricted by poverty.

(2) To provide courses so as to ensure that women gain entry into fields from which they have been traditionally excluded.

(3) To identify where and what kind of job opportunities are appearing in courses of the growing industrialization and modernization of the country.

(4) To consciously equip students to function as responsible citizens and self confident and responsible individuals.

(5) To advance the quality of education for women. The courses and facilities at the University are designed accordingly.

This Women's University has served the women in distress and endowed their lives with grace. By educating the women, the University has served society and the nation. The University has completed nearly eighty years of service now having commendably lived upto its chosen motto : "enlightened woman is a source of infinite power".

ANNEXURE 1
FACULTYWISE COURSES

1. Faculty of Arts, Faculty of Fine Arts, and Faculty of Social Sciences, unique Certificate Courses in Light Music, Post-graduate Diploma in Travel and Tourism, Proficiency in Music, B.A., M.A., M.Phil., Ph.D. are the degrees under the Arts Stream.
2. Faculty of Commerce: Under this Faculty B.Com. degree, Ph.D. and Post-Graduate Diploma in Banking are the courses.

3. Faculty of Home Science : (1) Certificate in Home Science, (2) Diploma in Home Science, (3) Post-Graduate Diploma in Food Service Management, (4) Communication and Media Development, (5) Dietetics, (6) Hospitality Administration, (7) Post-Graduate Diploma in Consumer Services, (8) Early Childhood Education, (9) Computer Aided Textile Designing, (10) Sports Science and Nutrition, (11) M. Phil. and (12) Ph.D.
4. Faculty of Education: Post-Graduate Diploma in Science Education, B.Ed., M.Ed., B.Ed., (Special education), M.Phil. in Education, Ph.D. in Education.
5. Faculty of Nursing - B. Sc. Nursing, M.Sc. Nursing, Ph.D..
6. Faculty of Library and Information Science: B.Lib. Science, M.Lib. Science, Ph.D..
7. Faculty of Technology : Diploma in Commercial and Secretarial Practice, Medical Laboratory Technology, Pharmacy, Dress Making & Fashion Co-ordination, Interior Design, Food Technology, ELectronics, B. Pharma, M. Pharma., Post-Graduate Diploma Course in Computer Science and Applications.
8. Faculty of Science : Post-Graduate Diploma in Analytical Chemistry, M.S.C. (Analytical and Medical Chemistry, M.S.C. (Chemistry).

WOMEN AND DISTANCE EDUCATION

JAMUNA THIAGARAJAN

The evolution of distance education as a global phenomenon itself comprises an interesting study. The aim of this article is to examine how distance-education serves the cause of women's education with special reference to our institutions, especially when this decade has been witnessing a spurt in activities which highlight women's development and education. Before focusing on the theme, it may be appropriate here to examine the salient features of distance education as this new concept needs to be continuously instilled in the minds of the public.

Distance learning lends itself to a variety of interpretations which empowers it as a concept. "Distance education" is an umbrella term which indicates the tangible distance between the learner and the teacher where the process of teaching and learning is not confined within the four-walls of the classroom any more. With its horizontal mobility, distance education transcends the barriers of time, space, sex, creed, community and religion, thus breaking the myth of elitism in conventional higher education which is rigid and restrictive.

Kevin Smith, former President of the International Council for Distance Education, attributes the following factors for the emergence of distance education:

1. Failure of traditional programmes to cater to the changing educational needs.
2. Need for democratising the educational process.
3. Consequential increase in numbers and categories of educational consumers.
4. Wider acceptance of the new communication-technology,

shrinking resources and a right to maintain the status quo, intertwined with challenges posed by the political, social and economic demands also facilitated its growth.

To sum up, in terms of human relations distance education would mean new forms of interaction between the teachers and the taught, in physical terms it would mean transcending the physical confines of the classroom, in temporal terms it would mean a flexible learning schedule and in curricular terms individualised and diversified learning sequences.

It is now felt that if the deficiencies and inadequacies of our educational system are to be corrected, there is a need to strengthen the non-formal system as a parallel and an alternative to the conventional system of education. Distance education is a properly blended product of formal and non-formal systems of education and this will be an answer to the ills that afflict our educational system.

In many cases, distance education adopts an integrated multimedia approach using print materials, broadcasting, audio-visual aids, tutorial system, study centres, contact programmes and summer-schools. Its strategies are so formulated that the learner becomes the pivot around whom the whole system is built. In order to establish the learner's autonomy there is a conceptual shift from the "teacher teaching" to the "learner learning" and the same is attributed to a "copernican revolution" in education. This system not only democratises access to learning but also cultivates respect for one's background while it facilitates the growth of better self-confidence and self-esteem in the learners as it provides an academically respectable education.

It may be of interest to know how some distinguished personalities felt about distance education. While delivering the first convocation address of the Andhra Pradesh Open University, Justice Pathak, (formerly chief Justice of the Supreme Court of India) expressed his view that he was quite optimistic about the constructive role of distance education in broadening the qualitative base of our people as we step into the twenty first century. Hon'ble Francis Fox, formerly minister for communications, government of

Canada, while delivering the inaugural address of the 12th World Conference of the International Council for Distance Education in Vancouver in 1982 pointed out that in Canada they have also recognised that in today's society, education is a life-long process that must serve children in their classrooms, farmers in their fields and workers in their factories. Today even the senior executives must be re-educated on a regular basis to keep abreast of technological changes.

When effectively implemented, distance education can cater to millions of people from all strata of society especially women, who are considered to be the weaker section. Women's education under the conventional system has been at a low ebb for reasons well-known. But distance learning has come as a boon to help them acquire new skills to enhance their status.

A look at the following statistics may well throw more light on the fact that women are indeed the beneficiaries of this dynamic system of education. These statistics show the percentage of women admitted in the academic year 1988-89 (i) in the under graduate course (U.G) in both English Medium (E.M) and Tamil Medium (T.M), (ii) in the course offered under the Open University System (OUS), in post graduate courses (P.G) both media and (iv) professional courses of the Institute of Correspondence Education (ICE) of the University of Madras.

ENROLMENT OF WOMEN IN THE INSTITUTE OF CORRESPONDENCE EDUCATION (ICE) OF MADRAS UNIVERSITY FOR THE YEAR 1988-89 AND 89- 90.

	1988-89			1989-90		
	Female	Total	% of Women Learners	Female	Total	% of Women Learners
	1	2	3	4	5	6
Undergrduate Courses						
B.A. HIST (E.M)	400	802	49.8	346	641	53.0
(T.M)	994	2290	43.5	1322	2658	49.0

Contd.

	1	2	3	4	5	6
B.A.ECO (E.M)	332	724	45.8	384	825	55.0
(T.M)	391	1006	38.5	466	1116	41.0
B.A. PSY (E.M)	92	205	44.8	76	185	41.0
(T.M)	33	104	31.7	40	120	33.0
B.A.I.M (E.M)	32	56	57.1	19	34	55.0
(Indian						
Music (T.M)	20	40	50.0	19	38	50.0
B.A. TAMIL	215	780	66.0	597	866	68.0
B.A. ENGLISH	580	879	65,9	609	940	64.0
B.A. LIT	738	1114	66.2	1113	1558	72.0
B.Sc (MATHS)						
(E.M)	497	1385	35.8	572	1411	40.0
(T.M)	576	1862	30.9	348	657	52.0
B.Com. (E.M)	1628	3662	44.4	1711	1411	40.0
(T.M)	576	1862	30.9	1711	3510	48.0
B.A. (Geo)(E.M)	29	63	46.0	26	74	35.0
(T.M)	37	73	50.6	26	74	35.0
Open University System						
B.A. HIS.(E.M)	433	1243	34.8	410	1113	35.6
(T.M)	2519	3512	28.2	1026	3513	29.2
B.A. ECO (E.M)	150	658	22.7	143	601	23.4
(T.M)	111	645	17.2	140	706	29.6
B.A.ECO (E.M)	150	658	22.7	143	601	23.4
(T.M)	111	645	17.2	140	706	29.6
B.A. PSYCHO(E.M)	41	144	28.4	41	118	33.9
(T.M)	25	93	26.8	13	23	56.5
B.A. Ind. Mus(E.M)	8	16	50.0	28	60	46.2
(T.M)	51	90	56.6	18	37	48.9
B.A. TAMIL	188	406	46.3	172	444	38.2

Contd.

	1	2	3	4	5	6
B.A. ENGLISH	288	639	45.0	297	602	49.2
B.Sc. MATHS (E.M)	78	393	19.8	54	237	22.8
(T.M)	39	137	28.4	13	42	33.1
B.Com (E.M)	344	1768	19.4	272	1191	23.0
(T.M)	77	713	10.7	48	430	11.7
B.LITT	625	1282	48.7	640	1321	49.1
Post-Graduate Courses						
M.A. (HIST) (E.M)	624	1132	55.1	551	923	55.1
(T.M)	448	1783	25.1	384	1493	25.1
M.A. ECO	540	1275	42.3	603	1350	44.0
M.A. POL. SCI	128	1500	25.6	84	399	21.3
M.A. PUB-ADMN	492	1532	32.1	439	1213	36.2
M.A. DEF. STUDIES	27	292	9.2	13	157	8.4
M.A. TAMIL	565	1311	43.0	430	985	44.5
M.A. ENG	899	1480	60.7	809	1300	62.5
M.COM	1103	3177	34.7	1306	3471	34.2
Professional Courses						
B.ED (E.M)	2447	4502	54.5	2098	3463	60.0
(T.M)	1046	2441	42.0			
M.ED.	396	983	40.0			
B.L.I.S.	110	353	32.2	404	1079	37.0
M.L.I.S.	227	522	43.5	120	416	28.0
C.L.I.S. (E.M)	54	261	20.5	202	555	36.0
(T.M)	100	350	14.2	178	824	21.0

It may be worthwhile examining a piece of information furnished by the Assistant Registrar of the Examination wing of this institute, in this context. Out of 25000 learners who had registered to write their examination in Madras in May 1989, 50% are women and it was rather difficult for him to arrange suitable venues for women in the city. This fact also indicates the seriousness of women who are definitely motivated to improve their qualifications.

Distance education administrators of today witness new scenes emerging in their set-up. Instead of parents taking care of the children, it is the grown-up children who take care of their parents' education in the institutes, like bringing lunch for their mothers who are attending contact programmes or coming to the institute to collect their mothers's study materials. Mothers with infants in their arms is a familiar scene. It may be even more amazing to learn about a retired officer bringing his 55-year old wife to admit her in M.A (English Literature) after making her complete B.A. (English) in an open university. These changing facets of the Institutes bear ample testimony to the fact that women are indeed the beneficiaries of this flexible system of education.

It is not necessary that women are always at the receiving end, they are also at the helm of affairs in the realm of distance education. At the international level a vital role is being played by Women's International Network (WIN) of the International Council for Distance Education (ICDE). Apart from their role in the deliberations in the ICDE, WIN plays yet another meaningful role in organising regional and national seminars to sensitise women's groups in distance education and contributing notably to research in distance education. A *Newsletter* of this body is circulated widely and a real networking is achieved amongst the women in Distance Education. A specific activity deserves mention here viz that of the former chairperson of WIN Ms. Liz Burge's successful experiment in audio teleconferencing as an interactive mode for a distance education-class. It should be noted that she willingly shares her experience and research papers with her colleagues around the world. The Indian branch of WIN had organised a national seminar on women in distance education in Madras (1988) to help them develop professionally.

In most institutions of distance education in India, there are women faculty members in administrative posts. The commendable service of the local women academics in conducting the contact programmes or evaluation of examinations is in no way negligible.

The above facts reveal that the participation of women in distance education has been really significant. Women who are aspiring to improve their status, do seek avenues in distance education successfully and are able to establish their own independent identities.

There is no doubt they are being equally benefited by the conventional courses offered by distance education institutes, but the real challenge to respond to the need of women's education lies in the hands of the distance education institutes. It is for them to design innovative, imaginative and creative need-based courses for the real development of women both rural and urban, at every level. Courses for employment, enrichment as well as enlightenment need to be carefully designed by them and offered to large sections of women. Surveys and researches conducted by various agencies should be taken into consideration for this purpose. If the national and state governments are seriously envisaging women's development, distance education should be exploited to the fullest advantage of the recipients as it is cost-effective. Various development agencies should be brought together and their coordinated efforts are bound to yield fruits in this direction.

Perhaps the following study of profiles of the cross-section of a few women-learners in the Institute of Correspondence Education of Madras University may further emphasise their enthusiasm and desire to utilise this channel for their self enhancement or development.

The first profile is that of a learner who is employed in the social forestry scheme. She hails from the Narikurava community (Scheduled Tribe). A keen student of B.A. (Economics) through distance education, she hopes to get a better job after completing her degree. She seems to be a tireless-worker and wants to take up the rehabilitation of her community.

The second learner is a housewife. After the sudden demise of her husband, a top official in the railways, she joined the institute and completed her M.A. (History). She has also obtained her B.Ed. through correspondence and is now employed in the railway school.

A third is a widow working in one of the city school libraries with her B.A. (Sanskrit). Through this Institute she completed both her B.Sc. (Maths) degree and Bachelor of Library and Information Science (BLIS) which helped her to get the post of a full-fledged librarian in her school.

The fourth one is a spectacular account of young girl who, after completing her B.A.. degree in a city college, completed her Master's degree in history in this Institute while doing her diploma course in Journalism. A top-ranker in the All India Competitive examinations she has been absorbed in the Indian Foreign Service.

The case of the fifth one, is that of brilliant young student of B. Com., of a local college. When her father was transferred to Calcutta she had joined this institute in B.Com. final and completed her degree with merit. She has simultaneously completed her Chartered Accountancy alongwith her degree.

The sixth, student is a young blind professional musician who is now doing her B.A. (Indian Music). She is also employed in the All India Radio.

Perhaps a unique example is that of the seventh learner who already had a Ph.D in economics to her credit. She has now joined MEd course in the institute.

Still another typical example is that of a rural elementary school teacher who was able to complete her B.A. in history from this Institute and is likely to complete her B.Ed shortly. There will be a definite enhancement in her status.

Orginally enrolled in the B.Com. course several years ago, a learner migrated to the US after marriage and was employed in a bank there. She returned to India to write and complete her B.Com degree. Now she proposes to do her M.Com to enhance her job prospects.

The above profiles are only a few random samples. There are thousands of such women from all strata of society enrolled here, with high aspirations, to better the prospects in their careers or lives. Would the distance education institutions both the Open Universities and institutes of distance/correspondence education of the conventional Universities in this country stand-up to their expectations? Would the Governments, both central and State, provide the necessary impetus to these institutions? These are certain vital issues which still remain unanswered.

What is needed is a concerted effort on the part of distance education institutions to provide a system that caters to the needs of the people looking for a second chance, especially women. There is an intense need for them to popularise this new concept by providing a scholarly basis for the theory and practice of distance education in this country. The following factors in the infrastructure need to be strengthened and given utmost priority:

i) new sophistication in the design and preparation of print-based materials.
ii) better support-systems to promote self-learning strategies
iii) an effective management of material production and distribution.

In all these areas, the gender perspective must remain central without which no support, be it moral or political or financial can be of any avail. This calls for real commitment and initiative.

INDIAN DISTANCE EDUCATION FOR WOMEN IN AN INTERNATIONAL FRAME

JANET JENKINS

This chapter takes the view that education has a relationship with national development, and looks from an international perspective at the contribution of distance education to women's development. There is a substantial demand amongst adult women the world over for education. It is evident, as we shall see, that distance education has had a considerable impact on women everywhere, mainly through providing greater access to education. There is still, however, much to be done. Many women are still denied access, and some who study find their experience unsatisfactory. The chapter reviews experience and research that throw light on such issues, and stresses the importance of women's involvement in designing education that is sensitive to the needs of women. Most reports of experience come from a few countries where distance education is well established; some institutions and countries are referred to quite often, as they are the only or best source of information, and any conclusions drawn are necessarily tentative. The case of India has been fully covered in the rest of the book, so this chapter reports on the rest of the world. The concluding section then examines the relevance of international experience to India and sketches a scenario for the future.

The demand for education comes from women everywhere, in rich or poor countries. The driving force is economic. Women, like men, work because they have to in order to support their families. A high proportion of women today all over the world are economically active. A recent survey (United Nations, 1989) shows that in about one-third of the countries for which figures are available, women form 40% or more of the total labour force—virtually full employment for women, allowing time off work for those with babies. Education for women is no longer, if it ever was, mainly a leisure time activity. Women take up educational opportunities for many reasons, but for many, almost certainly most, the benefits derived in present or future employment are a major factor.

Although the need for education is common to both men and women, women have particular disadvantages. First, they are less likely than boys to have gained full benefits from formal education. Less girls than boys, in almost every country in the world, go to university; more boys than girls complete school; and while almost every boy now goes to school at some time in his childhood, up to a quarter of the girls in the world's poorest countries never do so (United Nations, 1989). Today's inequities were even more pronounced when the women of today were children. Many women enter employment poorly educated and their lack of education not only condemns them to low status, poorly paid jobs but also closes the door on many opportunities for further training. So long as girls have unequal access to school, women will endure the consequences.

Home responsibilities further affect women's access to opportunities for employment and education. Most married women take the greater share of responsibility for caring for home, family and spouse. This obligation can limit the types of job a woman takes up and can limit her access to educational opportunities that will help her get a better one. In poorer countries women are the sole providers of income in up to one-third of families. Mothers who interrupt their paid employment or take on less demanding work in order to care for babies or infants usually do so at a point in their life when men of the same age are advancing rapidly in their careers. In such ways, women's disadvantage is compounded.

Distance education helps to make education and training more accessible to women. Distance education institutions may have a policy of open entry, allowing students without conventional entry qualifications to enrol. This is of particular value to women who failed to complete an earlier stage of education. Then, distance education allows people to study when and where they like, at a pace that suits them, and it provides tutorial support delivered at home.

Some have argued that study at home is an undesirable option for women who are already cut off from the outside world. Recent feminist analysis concludes otherwise:

> whilst women's isolation in the home is a problem that should not be down-played, criticisms that damn distance education as a further contributory cause are guilty of ignoring the material realities of women's lives. Every day women cope with the limitations placed on their lives by lack of money and time, by distance and geographical location, by inadequate childcare and public transportation systems. In this context, distance education is not a part of the problem. It is part of the solution (Coulter, 1989, pp 12-13).

The Educational Context

The importance of distance education for women is accentuated by the scarcity of other educational options. Since the disparity in access to education for girls is so pronounced and so long standing, it might be supposed that attempts to provide compensatory education for adult women were commonplace, at least in richer countries. Instead—to take Britain as a typical example—there are isolated examples of pre-university programmes that prepare women for higher education or community based projects that prepare them for employment. These are effective but affect very few women. Positive discrimination—the idea that because of past disadvantage special provision should be made—gets short shrift among educational policy makers (although ironically discriminatory quota arrangements are applied in education in some countries to induce various forms of racial or social 'balance'). The absence of special provision for women reinforces their disadvantage.

In a fast-changing context, there are differences in experience between generations which add complexity. In Britain, for example, only a few years ago many parents thought that education for girls as future housewives was a waste. Women who today are only in their mid-forties were, as girls, stopped by their parents from continuing their education beyond minimum school leaving age and even from taking up scholarships. These women must now compete in the job market with their own daughters, twenty years younger and better educated.

Massey University in New Zealand admits on its external programme both those with university entrance qualifications and those without, provided that they are over 25, under a scheme called provisional admission. A large number of women make use of this open entry facility. In the early 1980's one-third of all women external students enrolled under this procedure, while two-thirds of those provisionally admitted were women. It is suggested that the predominance of women taking up the option for provisional admission reflects social attitudes of earlier decades when girls were not encouraged to stay at school beyond the minimum age (Tremaine & Owen, 1984).

A woman returning to education in mid-life many years after leaving school is likely to face psychological difficulties in addition to educational ones. Lack of confidence is particularly common and distance education can, perhaps unexpectedly, provide reassurance. Rebecca Coulter again:

> Many women find distance-education learning, despite its flaws, considerably less threatening than other types of formal education. Women students often observed that they use distance-education courses to build up a confidence in their own skills before moving on to more traditional settings. Distance-education courses allow women to test themselves in relative privacy and in relatively non-threatening ways. Failure, if it comes, is not public (Coulter, 1989, pp. 15-16).

Conventionally taught programmes are also less convenient for many women. They may not be available at a time and place that suits women with work and family responsibilities. Distance education removes the constraint of attendance. It is therefore a potential catalyst for women. It can provide a plethora of opportunities from specialist training to longer programmes leading to degrees.

Women and Distance Education

In India, the government has stated its objective to improve women's participation in education:

> Education will be used as an agent of basic change in the status of woman. In order to neutralise the accumulated distortions of the past, there will be a well-conceived edge in favour of women. The National Education System will play a positive, interventionist role in the empowerment of women (Department of Education, 1986, p. 6).

Distance education is recognised in the same document as a 'powerful instrument' that can help achieve such ends. This section considers the extent to which distance education outside India has contributed to the achievement of similiar objectives. Higher education is examined first. It is, of course, in the area of higher education that distance education has so far made the greatest impact in India. The section goes on to consider other educational priorities for women, such as education directly related to employment and basic education.

A. *Higher Education*

The last few years have seen an enormous growth in the provision of distance education at university level throughout the world. There is now at least one Open University operating or planned in most countries of Asia, and throughout the world many countries now offer or are planning to offer distance education at tertiary level. Some opt for open universities, some for dual mode universities offering similiar programmes both face-to-face and at a distance, and others, like India, opt for both. In some countries university distance education is aimed primarily at adults, assuming that eligible school leavers will mostly attend conventional institutions, while other countries, often those with less well-developed educational facilities, admit both young and old to their open learning institutions. Open Universities hold particular attraction for countries with large populations, where the clientele for higher education is very great, while dual mode operations are preferred by countries with small populations. Both systems serve to expand access to education, for men as well as women. Figures of total numbers studying at university level using distance methods are hard to come by, but some estimate the total at more than ten million.

Most open universities attract a similar or slightly larger proportion of women students than conventional universities in the same country. At the British Open University, for example, just over 42% of undergraduates are women while in regular British universities they account for 41.5% of students (Kirkup, 1988). In Athabasca University, Canada, a provincial open university with a national intake, consistently attracts 60-62% women, while there are around 52% in conventional universities (Coulter, 1989). Everyman's University Israel has just over half its students female (Enoch, 1988), and the various distance education schemes in the Canadian province of British Columbia regularly expect between half and two-thirds of their students to be women (Sturrock, 1988). There are however one or two examples where women's participation is low. At the Fern Universitat, former West Germany's Open university, only about a quarter are women compared with 40% in regular tertiary education (Von Prummer and Rossie, 1988), while at the Dutch Open University only about one-third of the students are women (Boon and Joosten, 1988). Ideally all open universities should admit more women than men, to compensate for earlier disadvantage. There is little, however, to explain the differences between the examples above. Rebecca Coulter's comment on her own university speaks for all, when she says that 'no one has sytematically explored why distance education in the Athabasca University context is more appealing to women than men' (Coulter, 1989).

Where an imbalance between sexes occurs in participation in certain disciplines in the conventional education, that imbalance tends also to be reflected in distance education. Subject by subject breakdowns indicate that women tend to concentrate on less technical subjects, avoiding areas where they are traditionally underrepresented even if they could offer more scope for subsequent employment. At the British Open University in 1988, for example, over two-thirds of those studying the Arts foundation course were women, compared with just over a quarter of the Technology foundation course students, while over three quarters of those studying maths were men (Carter and Kirkup, 1991). It is somewhat disappointing that women do not participate equally in all disciplines. Once again distance education improves access for women at the same time as reinforcing the advantage that men already have.

Imbalance can be attacked through special programmes to support women who want to enter distance education. The case for such programmes still lacks general recognition. Efforts at the British Open University to improve women's representation have on occasions been ill received by the authorities as an apparent contravention of the principle of open access (Kirkup, 1988). One initiative however at the open university has had some success. In 1984 women staff at the open university formed an action group, Women into Science and Engineering (WISE), which has contributed to an improvement of women's enrolment in these subjects. Elsewhere in Pakistan the Allama Iqbal Open University has launched a matriculation programme for woman to bring more up to a level to start degree studies.

These two examples indicate two ways in which barriers to participation may be dismantled. The matriculation programme helps women catch up academically, of particular importance in a country with a very low participation in formal school. The WISE group directs its efforts at recruitment, providing information and advice, arousing the interest of potential students with a special leaflet "Technology is for Women Too" and providing opportunities at the university open days to try hands-on computing (Carter and Kirkup, 1991). But in any institution such special programmes for women compete with others for resources, and a convincing case must be made in their support. A recent small scale local scheme in Britain, for example, to help women to prepare for the open university's social science foundation course 'takes up an inordinate amount of time per student recruited, even if most of the ... people eventually enter higher education' (Mills, 1990). Without criteria for evaluating access courses, such judgements will inevitably be made.

It would be disappointing to find that once women have taken up the opportunity offered by distance study, they are more likely to give up before completion. Unfortunately there are indications that this is sometimes the case:

> One factor which causes students to discontinue their distance education is the initial misjudging of the required time and the workload on the one hand and the available spare time on the other hand. At first glance this affects both women and men but closer analysis shows that women are experiencing distinctly more pressure than men because they are not only affected by work commitments but also by their parenting and homemaker responsibilities (von Prummer, Kirkup & Spronk, 1988).

Research begins to offer some insight into how to make distance study more sensitive to women's needs. A recent comparative study of male and female students at the British Open University and the Fern Universitat aimed to identify factors impeding women's successful study:

> Despite organizational differences between the two institutions, the results from the two surveys show some striking similarities in the answering patterns of women in both institutions. There appears to be a pattern of preference among women for shared learning .... Women distance education students in the study were more interested than men in elements of interactive learning, and more inclined to make use of local study centres to obtain this. We suggest that our findings have

> positive implications for the design of local support systems for distance education students, in order to optimise the learning environment for women, and we question whether the concept of independence in distance education is modelled on male learning styles (Kirkup and von Prummer, 1990, p. 10).

In a number of cases, women's preference for shared learning is recognised. For example, Diana Carl of Mount Saint Vincent University in Canada (incidentally the first women's university in the Commonwealth) reports that in designing the curriculum for distance courses:

> An important consideration is to ensure that students accomplish some of the coursework outside of the home, preferrably in the company of others who are either taking the same course or who are interested in the content. Women are encouraged to learn in groups, either at home or in workplaces, and to support each other (Carl, 1988).

The introduction of strategies to give women better support depends largely on two factors: the presence of women within the institutions who are willing and powerful enough to act as prime movers; and institutional flexibility, in respect of entry requirements, programme design and implementation, and provision of support.

B. *Education for employment*

Distance education started in the nineteenth century with correspondence courses to train office workers in shorthand and book-keeping. Although recently somewhat overshadowed by the aura of open universities, it remains of great importance for the continuing professional education of those already at work and for training people for new jobs. Traditional areas like accountancy are still catered for, but distance education is also increasingly used for continuing and initial training for professionals such as teachers, nurses, doctors, lawyers and engineers. It is also used extensively for technical and vocational training.

One of the components of much professional and vocational education at a distance is practical work, on the job training, group seminars or residential courses. It may be compulsory for students to attend such sessions. It is a challenge to distance teaching institutions to make arrangements for such sessions that suit as many students as possible. It is necessary to provide facilities and supervision in a form, time and place accessible to distance learners.

Women students are likely to have greater difficulty than men in attending practical sessions. The following comments indicate the difficulties women have attending study centres. The comments, collected in Britain and Germany (Kirkup and Von Prummer, 1990), highlight problems of cost, travel, family responsibility and demands of employment and are relevant everywhere:

> I only attended twice. My son did not like being left alone at night . A sitter would cost ten pounds per evening.
>
> The study centre is 19 miles away and my husband would have to take me and pick me up.
>
> During the week the study centre is open while I'm at work, and on Saturdays my family needs me.

The conflict between home, work and study responsibilities is particularly strong when attendance at a centre is a compulsory element of course work. Not only is it difficult for many women to accommodate all their various responsibilities; they may also be tired by their day-to-day activities that group interaction is stressful (Burge and Lenskyj, 1990).

Such problems are commonplace. Others are less usual, but nonetheless critical to those who experience them. Some women endure harassment or ridicule from their husbands or members of their families if they try to study. For some, travel is dangerous, particularly after dark. For others cultural or religious constraints may inhibit participation in practical sessions, especially in a group of mixed sex.

Professions where in-service courses are widely offered at a distance include some which attract a high proportion of women, such as teaching and nursing. It is therefore critically important to make arrangements for face-to-face or practical sessions that suit women. To be sucessful, programmes may need to be designed to take into account women's requirements. Goroka Teachers College in Papua New Guinea, for example, offers at a distance an Advanced Diploma in teaching for high school teachers. The programme incorporates residential sessions. Many of the students are women and in a new experimental programme the residential sessions have been rearranged to suit their needs, with six short (one week) sessions a year:

> As a result of this scheduling change, women who were single heads of households who would not have been able to leave their families for the longer [six week] sessions have been able to attend. In addition, women on maternity leave... were able to participate.... Since Papua New Guinea promotes breast feeding as the best means of nourishing infants, it was not clear what impact this would have on nursing mothers' participation ... the women bring their babysitters (who would normally care for the children at home while the mothers were teaching their classes) with them to the site of the residential sessions (Simpson, 1990).

In Thailand about 70% of the doctors work in large cities and medical care in the countryside depends on nurses, mostly women. Although nursing personnel are more usually staffed by lower grade personnel, while fully qualified profesional nurses are concentrated in urban areas. The Sukhothai Thammathirat Open University (STOU) has since 1984 offered a BSc programme in nursing for underqualified nurses, to help raise the standards of health care in rural areas. The challenge of providing supervised clinical practice for rural nurses has been enormous. Several Thai universities collaborate in the programme with STOU, and tutors must travel on occasions to rural community hospitals to conduct the practice sessions. This makes the nursing programme more expensive than degree courses in other more conventional institutions.

So, what is to be done? We need to focus more on the content of distance education and its relevance for women.

In this section we examine more closely the process and content of distance education for women. This is of importance since:

> We know that the female experience of education differs from the male experience. That difference cannot be explained adequately by arguments about inherent male and female characteristics, but rather by the impacts of very early gender-based socialization, the consequent sets of achievement expectations, and conditions of schooling. 'Women's ways of knowing' and some of their preferred ways of learning are challenging educators to rethink how they can help women learn (Burge 1988).

As this chapter has made clear, work in distance education which looks specifically at women's issues is rare. We are however beginning to assemble a sketchy understanding of women's experience and we can draw a few tentative conclusions about the types of distance courses and styles of presentation that women prefer.

First, there is no doubt that there is a demand for special distance courses for women. Conventionally taught courses that help women gain access to higher education are always popular, and it will be of interest to watch the progress of the recently introduced distance taught matriculation programme for women in Pakistan. Distance courses in Women's Studies are now offered by about half a dozen universities outside India and in all cases there has been consistently high demand.

Next, in all distance education, more attention needs to be paid to preparing materials that show sensitivity to women as well as men. Many course materials contain unintentional bias. Content analysis of illustrations in some Kenyan courses, for example, produced startling results. In a distance training programme for adult educators men and boys were shown in pictures three times more often than women and girls:

> Of all the units studied in this course, psychology was the most biased. As might be expected, men are everywhere: they are on the way to the market, they are on the farm, on the plains, in adult classes and in a smithy, busily digging, instructing, herding, attacking, studying and making weapons. As also might be expected, women are carrying water, cooking and doing domestic chores. Only one woman is doing something different. She is reading (Matiru & Gachuhi 1988)

Major publishers ask their authors to follow guidelines for non-exist writing, but it seems that few distance education institutions follow suit.

The method and mode of study should also take into account women's needs. We have already noted that women respond well to styles of learning that are non-competitive and seen how group study, particularly when groups are homogeneous and single sex, can be used to provide support. In some circumstances women may prefer to study alone at home, especially if the alternative is to study in a mixed-sex group. A writer from Papua New Guinea argues:

> The competitiveness of face-to-face education is discouraging to women. Women may gain more through distance education precisely because it allows them to study as quiet learners. In home study, there is no visible domination by male students, as is the case in face-to-face learning (Mandie-Filer 1988).

We may also consider the media that are used. Earlier it was suggested that women may be disadvantaged by greater use of computers in distance education. On the other hand audio- cassettes are particularly popular with women who can listen and learn while doing household chores (Coulter 1989). And of course radio programmes are often used to reach and inform women, whether or not they can read.

Suggestions for gender-sensitive education will only be implemented if there is pressure for action from women. If pressure is to be informed by research, then women's studies courses can provide a base for the research to take placc. Such courses at Athabasca University and the British Open University led to findings which suggested changes. Pressure could be more effective if it comes from women in positions of responsibility. Ross Paul, currently president of a major Canadian University, believes that far more women should be promoted to senior positions, not only because they deserve the opportunity, but also because of the impact they will have on styles of leadership and the way decisions are made (Paul 1990). He observes that women are better listeners than men, more sensitive to the feelings of others, and less competitive than men. He also suggests that when men work with women their behaviour changes and 'they become better listeners and more thoughtful about the impacts of their decisions'.

The development of an inter-university project from Australia lends support to such views. In 1983 three Australian universities developed a joint Women's Studies Major programme, and it has since been offered and taught jointly by all three. Collaborative ventures are notoriously difficult to sustain and a 1987 evaluation examined the factors contributing to the success of this particular project. One of the evaluators, Louise Moran, concludes that the feminist approaches of the partners were critical:

> The Major highlights conditions conducive to effective collaboration - trust, communication, and esteem among partners; a willingness to compromise; and the presence of student demand that adequate operational resources. Together they suggest that feminist values of consensus, collective action rather than competition and sensitivity to others have much to offer distance educators pursuing inter-institutional collaboration. (Moran 1990).

In conclusion a policy for women needs women to make it.

Towards a women's system

Distance education has recently taken a great leap forward in India. It was slow to get an open university, compared with many other countries, but has rapidly become a leader in a new phase of distance education, which promotes collaboration and networking. India with its four operational open universities is attempting to develop its own elaborate network with a national open university system, a model for those who are attempting to collaborate internationally. India is still top heavy in distance education, with most activities at university level. But there is more at other levels than is at first obvious, and with the recent establishment of the National Open School there are now facilities to follow a complete course of education at a distance.

Open learning in India incorporates a number of features which are of special value to women. It is open as to entry requirements, flexible as to the pace and period of study, and provides a choice of syllabus options. The support provided through audiovisual media and study centres is also available on a flexible basis. All these features make the new Indian distance education institutions more attractive to women.

This more open style of distance education does no more than offer an environment more conducive to study for women. There are a few programmes which make special provision for women, notably those offered by SNDT Women's University, Bombay. But by and large India has not yet developed the positive, pro-active approach to education for women that evidence from elsewhere suggests is desirable.

It would not be difficult to introduce such an approach. Using examples from India itself and from other countries mentioned in this chapter, it is possible to envisage a complete distance education system, designed with women in mind, although it need not be closed to men. It could include literacy classes, taught conventionally but based around video programmes and literacy primers. A notable example of such a video series is the Hindi language film serial for adult women learners, *Khilti Kaliyan*, produced in 1988.

The series motivates women to learn to read through a powerful depiction of the value of literacy in village life, and at the same time shows women helping other women. Once literate, women can follow primary and secondary level programmes by correspondence. While the National Open School, complemented by state institutions using state languages, can now provide opportunities for such women, experience quoted from, for example, Canada suggests that all-women study groups may have an important role in building up confidence. Similarly, vocational and professional programmes might attract more students with all- women groups; an experiment could be tried with the IGNOU management programme, which currently enrole a predominantly male clientele. International experience presents a convincing case for extensive study group support for women. Similarly, there is a role for courses of special interest to women. A few vocational programmes in India such as IGNOU's Diploma in Food and Nutrition are aimed specifically at women. Undergraduate programmes attract a fair number of women, helped by the special access programme offered by SNDT and preparatory courses offered by IGNOU for such programmes for application oriented courses may perhaps help women in efforts to establish themselves in a career. It would not take much to strengthen all these and similar together, so that women, whatever their age, circumstances or previous experience, can find a means to a full achieved? Can India build on the experience reported in this chapter and provide a model of distance education for women for the rest of the world?

REFERENCES

Boon, Jo and Gerry Joosten (1988), 'A Reconsideration of the Attraction of the Dutch Open University for Female Students' in Faith (ed) pp. 254 - 263

Boontong, Tassana (1990), 'Distance Education for Nursing Personnel in Thailand', paper prepared for World Health Organization South-East Asia Region and Sukhothai Thammathirat Open University Inter-Country Workshop on Distance Education for Nursing Personnel and Other Health Workers, Thailand, October 1990

Burge, Elizabeth (1988), 'Foreword' in Faith (ed) pp vii - xiv

Burge, Elizabeth and Helen Lenskyj (1990), 'Women Studying in Distance Educational: Issues and Principles' in *Journal of Distance Education* Vol V No 1 pp. 20 - 37

Carl, Diana R (1988), 'Atlantic Canada Perspectives - Mount Saint Vincent University' in Faith (ed) pp 108 - 114

Carter, Ruth and Gill Kirkup (1991), 'Redressing the Balance: Women into Science and Engineering' in *Open Learning* Vol 6 No 1 pp 56 - 58

Coulter, Rebecca (1989), 'Women in Distance Education: Towards a Feminist Perspective' in Robert Sweet (ed) *Post-Secondary Distance Education in Canada*, Athabasca, Canada, Athabasca University & Canadian Society for Studies in Education.

Croft Marian, Ian Mugridge, John S Daniel, Allan Herschield (eds) (1990), *Distance Education: Development and Access,* Caracas, International Council for Distance Education.

Department of Education (1986), *National Policy on Education - 1986*, New Delhi, Ministry of Human Resource Development.

Enoch, Yael (1988), 'Women as Distance Learners in Israel' in Faith (ed) pp 67 - 81

Faith, Karlene (ed) (1988), *Toward New Horizons for Women in Distance Education - International Perspectives*, London and New York, Routledge.

Keough, Erin (1988), 'Atlantic Canada Perspectives - Memorial University at Newfoundland' in Faith (ed) pp 114 - 117

Kirkup, Gill (1988), 'Sowing Seeds: Initiatives for Improving the Representation of Women (United Kingdom)' in Faith (ed) 287 - 312

Kirkup, Gill and Christine von Prummer (1990), 'Support and Connectedness: the Needs of Women Distance Education Students' in *Journal of Distance Education* Vol V no 2 pp 9 - 31.

Koul B N and J Jenkins (eds) (1990), *Distance Education: a Spectrum of Case Studies*, London, Kogan Page.

Mandie-Filer, Angela (1988), 'Women in Papua New Guinea: Distance Education as a means for Educational Advancement' in Faith (ed) pp 129 - 136

Matiru, I Barbara and Debbie Gachuhi (1988), 'Female Imagery in Course Materials: Kenya' in Faith (ed) pp 137 - 151.

Mills, Roger (1990), 'Access for Adults to Higher Education - The Role of Distance Education' in Croft M et al (eds)

Moran, Louse (1990), 'Inter-institutional Collaboration: The Case of the Australian Inter-University Women's Studies Major' in *Journal of Distance Education* Vol V No 2 pp 32 - 48

Paul, Ross H (1990), *Open Learning and Open Management,* London & New York, Kogan Page & Nichols

Simpson, Norma L (1990), 'Combining Distance Education with Residential Instruction to Up-grade Secondary Teachers in Papua New Guinea' in Croft M et al (eds)

Sturrock, June (1988), 'Canada: The West Coast' in Faith (ed) pp 24 - 38

Tremaine, Marianne and Judy Owen (1984), 'The Female Majority: Women who study extramurally' in *Teaching at a Distance* No. 25, pp 45 - 50

Unesco (1988), *Compendium of Statistics on Illiteracy,* Paris, Unesco

United Nations Centre for Social Development and Humanitarian Affairs (1989), *1989 World Survey on the role of Women in Development,* New York, United Nations

von Prummer, Christine and Ute Rossie (1988), 'Gender-related Patterns in Choice of Major Subject or Degree Course at Fern Universitat (West Germany)' in Faith, pp 39 - 66

Warr, David (1990), 'Functional Project in Rural Areas, Pakistan' in Koul and Jenkins (eds) pp 195 - 197

Young, Michael, Hilary Perraton, Janet Jenkins and Tony Dodds (1980), *Distance Teaching for the Third World,* London, Boston and Henley, Routledge & Kegan Paul

SELECT BIBLIOGRAPHY

NEELA JAGANNATHAN

Al-Rawaf, Haya Saad & Simmons, Cyril (1992): "Distance higher education for women in Saudi Arabia: Present and proposed". In *Distance Education,* 13 (1), 1992. 65-80.

Belenky, M. (1986): "Women's ways of knowing: The development of self, voice and mind". New York: Basic Books.

Boon, J. & Joosten, G. (1988): "A reconsideration of the attraction of the Dutch Open University for female students". In *Toward new horizons for women in distance education: International perspectives* ed. by Karlene Faith. London: Routledge. 254-263.

Bray, C. (1990): "Cyborgs, nurses and distance education: A feminist science fiction". In *Journal of Distance Education.* 5, 2, Fall 1990. 59-69.

Brunner, C. (1991): "Gender and distance learning". In *Electronic links for learning - The Annals of the American Academy of Political & Social Science,* 514, March 1991. 133-45.

Burge, E.J. (1990): "Women as learners: Issues for visual and virtual classrooms". In *Canadian Journal for the Study of Adult Education,* 4 (2), 1-23.

Burge, E.J. & Lenskyj, H. (1990): "Women studying in distance education: Issues and principles". In *Journal of Distance Education,* 5 (1) Spring, 1990, 20-37.

Carl, D.R. et al. (1988): "Atlantic Canada perspectives". In *Toward new horizons for women in distance education: International perspectives* ed. by Karlene Faith. London: Routledge. 107-120.

Carter, R. & Kirkup, Gill (1991): "Redressing the balance: Women into Science and Engineering". In *Open Learning,* 6 (1), February 1991. 56-58.

Cole, Sue ed. (1989): "Women educating women: Exploring the potential of open learning". Cambridge: The National Extention College.

Coulter, R. (1989): "Women in distance education: A feminist perspective". In *Post-secondary distance education in Canada: Policies, practices and priorities* ed. by R. Sweet. Alberta: Athabasca University & Canadian Society for Studies in Education. 11-22.

Crocombe, M.T. et al. (1988): "Women in distance education at the University of the South Pacific". In *Toward new horizons for women in distance education: International perspectives* ed. by Karlene Faith. London: Routledge. 152-171.

Effeh, Eno (1991): "Determinants of the study patterns of female distant learners: An evaluative survey". In *Journal of Distance Education,* (2) Fall/Automne 1991, 58-63.

Enoch, Y. (1988): "Women as distance learners in Israel". In *Toward new horizons for women in distance education: International perspectives* ed. by Karlene Faith. London: Routledge. 67-81.

Erchler, M. (1988).: "Non-sexist research methods: A practical guide". Boston: Allen & Unwin.

Euler, Ajayi L. (1988): "Distance education: A necessity for Nigerian women". In *Proceedings of the fourteenth ICDE World Conference.* Oslo: ICDE. 16.

Evans, T. & Nation, D. (1989): "Critical reflection on distance education". London: Falmer Press.

Faith, Karlene (1988): "Naming the problem". In *Toward new horizons for women in distance education: International perspectives* ed. by Karlene Faith. London: Routledge. 3-18.

Faith, Karlene ed. (1988): "Toward new horizons for women in distance education: International Perspectives". London: Routledge.

Faith, Karlene & Coulter, Rebecca P. (1988): "Home study: keeping women in their place?". In *Developing Distance Education* ed. by D. Sewart & J.S. Daniel. Oslo: ICDE. 195-98.

Furler, L. & Scott, C. (1988): "Negotiating a new model for aboriginal teacher education: A case study". In *Toward new horizons for women in distance education: International perspectives* ed. by Karlene Faith. London: Routledge. 229-247.

Grace, M. (1991): "Gender issues in distance education: A feminist perspective". In *Beyond the text: Contemporary writing on distance education* ed. by T. Evans & B. King. Geelong, Victoria: Deakin University Press.

Griffen, A. (1986): "The female distance learner: Motivation, persistence and success in pre-degree English courses". In *Directions*, 8 (1 & 2) 1986, 87-92.

Harding, Sandra (1986): "The science question in feminism". Milton Keynes: Open University Press.

Harding, Sandra ed. (1987): "Feminism and methodology: Indiana and Milton Keynes". Indiana University Press & Open University Press.

Heiler, P. & Richards, W. (1988): "By print and post: Vocational training of isolated women". In *Toward new horizons for women indistance education: International perspectives* ed. by Karlene Faith. London: Routledge. 190-204.

Herbst, I. (1992): "Distance learning for women in the family period". INBJUDAN: Distansundervisning. June 1992.

Kirkup, Gill (1983): "Women's Studies "at a distance": The new Open University Course". In *Women's Studies International Forum* 6(3).

Kirkup, Gill (1986): "The feminist evaluator". In *New directions in educational evaluation* ed. by Ernest House. London: Falmer Press. 68-84.

Kirkup, Gill (1988a): "Considering the effect on women of an increased use of micro-computers in distance education". In *Proceedings of the fourteenth ICDE World Conference.* Oslo: ICDE. 9.

Kirkup, Gill (1988b): "Sowing seeds: Initiatives for improving the representation of women". In *Toward new horizons for women in distance education: International perspectives* ed. by Karlene Faith. London: Routledge. 287-312.

Kirkup, Gill (1989a) "Equal opportunities and computing at the Open University". In *Open Learning* 4, (1) February 1989. 3-8.

Kirkup, Gill (1989b): "Feminist research methodology". In *Women's International Network Newsletter* 10, Oslo. International Council for Distance Education.

Kirkup, Gill et al. (1991): "Home base computing for women students". In *Women into Computing - selected papers: 1988-90* ed. by G. Lovegrove. Springer-Verlag.

Kirkup, Gill & Von Pruemmer, C. (1990): "Support and connectedness: The needs of women distance education students". In *Journal of Distance Education* 5 (2), 1990, 9-31.

Koymen, U.S. (1988): "Women in Turkey and the potential for open learning". In *Toward new horizons for women in distance education: International perspectives* ed. by Karlene Faith. London: Routledge. 205-213.

Leonard, D. (1984): "The changing experience of women at the Open University". In *Breaking the Mould* ed. by M. Hughes & M. Kennedy.

Macaskill, J. (1988): "Teaching art at a distance in New Zealand". In *Toward new horizons for women in distance education: International perspectives* ed. by Karlene Faith. London: Routledge. 82-92.

Mandie, Filer, A. (1988): "Women in Papua New Guinea: Distance Education as a means for - educational advancement". In *Toward new horizons for women in distance education: International perspectives* ed. by Karlene Faith. London: Routledge. 129-136.

Mani, Gomathi (1988): "Women in distance education: Issues and prospects". Madras, India: Women's International Network of ICDE.

Mani, Gomathi et al. (1988): "The Indian experience". In *Toward new horizons for women in distance education: International perspectives* ed. by Karlene Faith. London: Routledge. 172-189.

Matiru, B. & Güchuhi, D. (1988): "Female imagery in course materials: Kenya". In *Toward new horizons for women in distance education: International perspectives* ed. by Karlene Faith. London: Routledge. 137-51.

Matiru, I.B. & Guchuhi, D. (1987): "The image of women and girls in distance education materials for secondary school courses in Kenya". In *Distance education - by design.* Alberta: Alberta Correspondence School. 1-13.

May, Susan, (1994): "Women's experiences as distance learners: Access and technology. In *Journal of Distance Education* IX (1), Spring, 1994. 81-98.

Mishra, S.K. (1992): "Empowerment of women through extension education". In *Kakatiya Journal of Distance Education* 1 (1), 1992, 114-21.

Oudshoorn, N. (1988): "Towards a more women-centred approach for distance education-curriculum". In *Toward new horizons for women in distance education: International perspectives* ed. by Karlene Faith. London: Routledge. 264-274.

Peacock, Geraldine et al. (1978): "New opportunities for women: A group entry project at Newcastel upon Tyne". In *Teaching at a Distance* 12, Summer 1978. 33-42.

Porter, P. (1986): "Gender and education in Geelong ". Victoria: Deakin University Press.

Pravda, Gisela (1991): "Women-friendly approaches to teaching and learning - An overview of selected papers presented on the occasion of the International Conference on "The Student, Community and Curriculum: International Perspectives in Open and Distance Learning at Cambridge from 10-13 September, 1991".

Ross, L.R. & Powell, (1990): "Licenceship between gender and success in distance education courses: A preliminary investigation". In *Research in Distance Education* 2 (2), 10-11.

Simpson, N.L. (1990): "Combining distance education with residential instruction to upgrade - secondary teacherrs in Papua New Guinea". In *Distance Education: Development and access* ed. by Marion Craft et al. Caracas: Universidad Nacional Abierta & ICDE. 124-26.

Sloper, D.W. (1990): "Meeting the needs of overseas postgraduate women students through flexible distance education". In *Distance Education* 11, (2) 1990. 266-86.

Smith, Dorothy E. (1983): "The everyday world as problematic: A feminist sociology". Milton Keynes, UK: Open University Press.

Smith, R. (1987): "Equal opportunities in management education and training?". In *Open Learning* 2 (3), November 1987. 36-39.

Sturrock, J. (1988): "Canada: The West-Coast". In *Toward new horizons for women in distance education: International perspectives* ed. by Karlene Faith. London: Routledge. 25-38.

Swarbrick, Ailsa (1980): "To encourage the others: Women studying technology". In *Teaching at a distance* 17, Spring 1980. 2-14.

Treamaine, Marianne & Owen, Judy (1984): "The female majority: Women who study extramurally". In *Teaching at a Distance* 25, Autumn 1984. 45-50.

Trivedi, J.H. (1989): "Women's development through distance education". In *ICDE Bulletin* 21, 1989, 17-22.

Van Dyke, Ruth (1991): "Equal opportunities guidelines for course materials". Milton Keynes: Open University.

Von, Pruemmer C. (1988): "Gender in distance education: Women and men studying at the West-German Fern Universitaet". In *Developing distance education* ed. by D. Sewart & J.S. Daniel. Oslo: ICDE. 372-74.

Von, Pruemmer C. (1986): "Women at the Fernuniversitaet: Gender related differences in students choice of degree programs". In *ICDE Bulletin* 11, May 1986. 42-50.

Von, Pruemmer C. et al. (1988): "Women in distance education". In *Developing distance education* ed. by D. Sewart & J.S. Daniel. Oslo: ICDE. 57-62.

Von, Pruemmer C. (1991): "Distance education and women in East Germany". In *The student, community and curriculum: International perspectives on open and distance learning* ed. by A. Tait. Cambridge: Open University & Empire State College of New York. 303-11.

Von Pruemmer, Christine & Rossie, U. (1988a): "Gender in distance education at the Fern Universitat". In *Open Learning* 3, (2) June 1988. Harlaw. Longman.

Von, Pruemmer, C. & Rossie, U. (1988b): "Gender-related patterns in choice of major subject or degree course at Fern Universitat". In *Toward new horizons for women in distance education: International perspectives* ed. by Karlene Faith. London: Routledge. 39-66.

Von, Pruemmer, C. & Rossie, U. (1990): "Women in distance education : Value of study centres and support services: Selected research fundings". Hogen: Basic Books.

Willen, B. (1988): "Distance education as a means of enhancing self-esteem among adult female students in Sweden". In *Toward new horizons for women in distance education: International perspectives* ed. by Karlene Faith. London: Routledge. 93-106.

Women's Studies Centre of Umea, (1993): "Feminist pedagogy and women friendly perspectives in distance education." In *Proceedings of WIN Working Conference* 10-13 June 1993. (Report no. 4)

NOTES ON CONTRIBUTORS

Asha S. Kanwar is a Professor of English at the Indira Gandhi National Open University. A British Council grant enabled her to obtain her Doctor of Philosophy at the University of Sussex, England where she wrote her doctoral thesis on British Marxism and the nineteenth century novel. Asha received a Fulbright fellowship in 1992 for research on fiction by African-American women writers which she conducted during her tenure at the English department, Iowa State University, Ames, Iowa. Asha is the author of two critical books entitled *The Novels of Virginia Woolf and Anita Desai* (New Delhi: Prestige, 1989) and *Fictional Theories and Three Great Novels* (New Delhi: Prestige, 1990). She has co-translated Ngugi wa Thiong'o's novel *Matigari* into Hindi (New Delhi: Atma Ram, 1991) and has edited *The Unforgetting Heart: An Anthology of Short Stories by African-American Women 1859-1993* (San Francisco: Aunt Lute, 1993).

Jamuna Thiagarajan had been the Deputy Director of the Institute of Correspondence Education, University of Madras. She has presented papers and participated in various national as well as international conferences.

Janet Jenkins has worked for over 25 years in open and distance learning as practitioner, manager and trainer. After grduating from the University of Cambridge, she worked at the National Extension College, Cambridge and then for the International College. During that period consultancy took her to over 20 countries and involved project development, mnagement and evaluation, staff training and materials development. She visited IGNOU on several occasions. In 1990 she joined the Commonwealth of Learning, Vancouver, as Senior Programme Officer to work on programmes of distance education in Commonwealth countries in South Asia, and on the development and implementation of COL's Commonwealth-wide programme of staff training in the techniques of distance education. She then moved to become the first Director of Programmes at the Open Learning Foundation, UK a collabortive network of over 20 British universities. Since October 1993 she has been working independently. She is currently Consultant in Distance Education to the Ministry of Education and Science, Mauritius.

B.K. Kamala obtained her Ph.D. in Botany from Osmania University, Hyderabad. She has completed Postgraduate Diploma in Distance Education from the Indira Gandhi National Open University, New Delhi. A teacher for two decades she is presently Deputy Director, Student Services and is incharge of a Study Centre for Women of the B.R. Ambedkar Open University, Hyderabad. Kamala has attended several national level seminars and worshops on various aspects of distance eduction and has also participated and presented papers in two international conferences on "Geopolitics of the Environment and the New World Order: Limits, Conflicts, Insecurity" at Paris and "Feminist Pedagogy and Women-friendly perspectives in Distance Education" at Umea, Sweden, June 1993.

Manjulika Srivastava is the Assistant Regional Director at the Bangalore Regional Centre of the Indira Gandhi National Open University. Previously, she has worked as a member of the editorial team in the *Times of India*, as a Research Associate in the Institute of Social Studies Trust and as a lecturer in History at the University of Delhi. Manjulika is the author of a book on advertising entitled '*Brand New*'. As one of the members of the editorial team of *Times of India*, she has contributed to four books and four magazines. She has conducted a survey in Karnataka region on the functioning of IGNOU and done extensive research in the area of distance education. In fact, she is doing her doctoral research in this area from the Jamia Millia Islamia University, New Delhi.

Mukta Prahlad is a Reader at the Department of Correspondence

Courses, Central Institute of English and Foreign Languages, Hyderabad.

Neela Jagannathan, holds M.A., MLIS and Ph.D. degrees from the University of Bombay. She was the first Librarian of the B.R. Ambedkar Open University (BRAOU), Hyderabad from 1983-87. Since 1987, she has held the posts of Deputy Librarian and Acting Librarian of the Indira Gandhi National Open University, (IGNOU) New Delhi. Neela is the joint-director of the "Directory of Women Studies Organisations in India" published by the Association of Indian Universities and the Commonwealth of Learning (COL), Vancouver, Canada. She has recently co-edited "Library Services to Distance Learners in the Commonwealth: A Reader" with Elizabeth F. Watson, Librarian of Learning Resources Centre, Barbados which will be published in 1995. At present, Neela is compiling "A Resource Directory of Women's Organisations in India", a project sponsored by COL in collaboration with IGNOU.

C. Pushpa Ramakrishna has a P.G. Diploma in English Studies and an M.Litt. from CIEFL. For about a decade she has been associated with different forms of Distance Education—Correspondence Institutes and Open Universities—in the capacity of a tutor, counsellor, coordinator, evaluator. She has prepared instructional materials for distance learners in both the print and non-print modes and has participated in seminars/conferences/workshops at the national and international levels. She is presently Deputy Director, Staff Training and Development, Dr. B.R. Ambedkar Open University, Hyderabad.

Renu Bhardwaj is a lecturer in the School of Humanities at Indira Gandhi National Open University. Though her Ph. D. is in English literature, her professional interests range in the area of instructional design and experiential taxonomy in distance education as also Women's Studies. After a distinguished career in administration, media and research, she taught in conventional and correspondence institutions before joining IGNOU in 1987. She has been invited as chairperson and panelist of ICDE's conferences and has been a guest speaker for a course on Adult Education for the students of Pennsylvania through satellite tele-conferencing. In India she is the co-founder of the Indian Society of Experiential Learning (I.S.E.L.) and helped organise the Third International Conference of Experiential Learning at Pondicherry. At present she is involved in research on design, implementation and evaluation of Experiential Taxonomy in Distance Education.

C. Sesharatnam is presently a Deputy Director at Dr. B.R. Ambedkar Open University, Hyderabad. Earlier she taught Chemistry at Anwar-Ul-Uloom College affiliated to Osmania University. She attended national and international seminars on Student Support Services. She has authored articles on distance education and coedited a book in Telugu on Open Universities.

Shobhita Jain obtained her Ph.D. degree at the Centre for the Study of Social Systems, Jawaharlal Nehru University New Delhi. She has held teaching and research assignments in India, Australia, the U.K. and the West Indies. During 1982-83 she was the Director of the Programmes for Women's Development at the Indian Social Institute, New Delhi. Having completed a research consultancy for FAO, Rome on Farm Forestry in Gujarat she worked as a Consultant with the Multiple Action Research Group, New Delhi. She is at present Reader in Sociology, IGNOU, New Delhi. Shobhita Jain's research publications include papers in *Social Action, Economic and Political Weekly, Relevant Sociology, The Eastern Anthropology and UNASYLVA and an article in Visibility and Power: Essays on Women in Society and Development*. She is also the author of a report - *Caste Studies of Farm Forestry and Wasteland Development in Gujarat, India* published by FAO Bangkok and a monograph *Sexual Equality, Workers in an Asian Plantation System.*

Uma Kanjilal has an M.A. in Economics from Kanpur University, and BLIS and MLIS from Delhi University. She has obtained Ph. D. in Library and Information Science from Jiwaji Unversity, Gwalior on her thesis titled 'Role of Library and Modern Information Technology in Distance Education (With Special Reference to India). She is a lecturer in the Faculty of Library and Information Science, Indira Gandhi National Open University, New Delhi, since 1989 where she has been involved in the planning and preparation of course materials for LIS programmes.

Uma Shekhar Vandse, is the Director of Department of Correspondence Courses and Distance Education at S.N.D.T. Women's University, Bombay. She has been the recipient of the Chancellor's award for her Ph. D. thesis 'Hymns in Marathi Literature'. Association of Commonwealth Universities had awarded her Senior Fellowship in Distance Education in 1987. Uma Vandse is the author of a critical study of Ravi Anil entitled 'Chirayouvan: Ek Abhyas'. She has translated the ICSSR Publication "Status of Women, 1988" and the Gujarati novel "Anagat" into Marathi. She has edited selections "Gadyanjali" and "Padyanjali" in 1990 and conducted a survey of distance learners 'Look Back-Look Forward' in 1989-90. Her book entitled "Marathi Stotra Kavya" is under print and she is writing a book on distance education.

M.D. Ushadevi has a Ph.D. from the University of Mysore. She has also obtained a Diploma in Distance Education and Diploma in Higher Education from the Indira Gandhi National Open University, New Delhi and was awarded a gold medal. She is an Assistant Professor at the Institute for Social and Economic Change, Bangalore. Her areas of specialisation include Educational Management and Administration, Curriculum Development, Distance Education and Higher Education. She has co-authored two books on Primary Education in Rural Areas and Adult Education. Ushadevi is the recipient of the Shastri Indo-Canadian Fellowship in Women in Development 1993-94 to carry out research in Distance Education with a special focus on women. She was also awarded the Ford Foundation Visiting Fellowship in 1994 and visited a few universities in USA to study women's participation in higher education through the distance delivery mode.

